Alphabet of the World

Chicana & Chicano Visions of the Américas

Alphabet of the World

Selected Works by Eugenio Montejo

∿

A Bilingual Edition

Translated by Kirk Nesset
Introduction by Wilfredo Hernández and Kirk Nesset

For Dwight,
Good luck with your
poetry — keep up that
writerly faith !
(Great to meet you
in Killeen !)

University of Oklahoma Press : Norman

This book is published with the generous assistance of the McCasland Foundation, Duncan, Oklahoma.

Library of Congress Cataloging-in-Publication Data

Montejo, Eugenio.
    [Selections. English & Spanish. 2010]
    Alphabet of the world : selected works / by Eugenio Montejo ; a bilingual edition translated by Kirk Nesset ; introduction by Wilfredo Hernández and Kirk Nesset.
        p. cm. — (Chicana & Chicano visions of the Américas ; v. 8)
    Includes bibliographical references and index.
    ISBN 978-0-8061-4148-0 (pbk. : alk. paper)
    1. Montejo, Eugenio—Translations into English.   I. Nesset, Kirk.   II. Title.
    PQ8550.23.O54A2   2010
    861'.64—dc22
                                                                            2010016583

Alphabet of the World: Selected Works by Eugenio Montejo, A Bilingual Edition is Volume 8 in the Chicana and Chicano Visions of the Américas series.

The paper in this book meets the guidelines for permanence and durability of the Committee on Production Guidelines for Book Longevity of the Council on Library Resources, Inc. ∞

1 2 3 4 5 6 7 8 9 10

Contents

Acknowledgments

I am grateful to a number of people who offered valuable input as this manuscript emerged. These generous readers and critics include Maria De Castro, Katrin Flechsig, Rosario Gonzales, Marta Llath-Barrera, Paul Raymond Martin, Barbara Riess, and Matthew Rose. Above all I am indebted to Wilfredo Hernández, my friend, colleague, and co-introducer, who was unswervingly giving and on hand every step of the way.

I am grateful as well to the editors of journals and periodicals in which most of these translations originally appeared—to Jeanne Leiby, especially, and to Sven Birkerts, Christopher Cox, Carol Ann Davis, Garrett Doherty, Jessica Faust-Spitzfaden, Ilya Kaminski, Martin Lammon, Jackson Lears, David Lynn, Fred Moramarco, Donna Perrault, Stephanie Volmer, and John Witte. The pieces first appeared in the following publications:

ABZ Magazine: "She Who Sleeps"
Agni: "Honor the Ass"
American Letters and Commentary: "The Grammar
    of Absence," "The Last Rooster," "Way Off in the
    Twentieth Century"
Apalachee Review: "Men Without Snow"
Arroyo: "The White Workshop," "Hamlet's Hour," "A Year"

Arts and Letters: "White Axe," "Waking Up," "Stars," "Here"

California Quarterly: "Delivery Room," "Coming Back"

Carolina Quarterly: "On This Street"

Chelsea: "*Letra Profunda*"

The Christian Science Monitor: "Poetry"

Cider Press Review: "Love Isn't Ours"

Cimarron Review: "Another Millennium"

Conduit: "House"

Crazyhorse: "My Lantern," "If I Return Again"

Denver Quarterly: "Guitar of the Horizon"

Good Foot: "Door"

Green Mountains Review: "Magic Life"

The Kenyon Review: "The Mill"

LIT: "On the Eve of Embarking," "Avenue Duque de Loulé"

Meridian: "Another Rain," "Song"

Michigan Quarterly Review: "Writing"

Mid-American Review: "I Believe," "Duration"

New American Writing: "Midnight," "Distant"

New England Review: "Alphabet of the World," "Written in Passing"

Northwest Review: "Hamlet, Act One," "Elegy on the Death of My Brother Richard," "Beyond Time," "My Father Returns and Sleeps, "The Other"

The Paris Review: "Winter Trees Cough Like Old Men"

Poetry International: "Toad," "Letters," "Here Again"

Potomac Review: "A Bird's *Terredad*"

Raritan: "In Forests of My Ancient Home," "I Speak and Unspeak," "El Dorado," "In the Time That Remains"

Rhino: "Snow"

Salt Hill: "Here on Earth," "The Last Bird"

South Carolina Review: "End of Rain"

Southern Humanities Review: "In Paradise"

The Southern Review: "September," "I Must Be Far Off," "The Notebook of Blas Coll"

Spoon River Poetry Review: "When My Statue Awakens"
Verse: "My Country on an Ancient Map"

"Winter Trees Cough Like Old Men" and "The Other"
reappeared in *Poetry Daily*.

Introduction

*Wilfredo Hernández
and Kirk Nesset*

The Venezuelan poet Eugenio Montejo died in June 2008, shortly after this book went into production. He passed away early, but in his sixty-nine years he had accomplished much. He was the author of ten books of poetry, including *Elegies, Death and Memory, A Few Words, Terredad, Farewell to the Twentieth Century,* and *The Scribe's Fable.* Numerous anthologies of his selected poems had appeared in his native country and abroad. He had also published five "heteronymic" volumes (by imaginary authors) and two books of essays. Montejo received Venezuela's National Literature Prize in 1998 and, later, two honorary doctorates of letters conferred by the University of Carabobo and the University of the Andes. He stands among his nation's canonized poets: Andrés Bello and Juan Antonio Pérez Bonalde from the nineteenth century and José Antonio Ramos Sucre from the early twentieth century. In 2004, he was awarded the Octavio Paz International Poetry and Essay Prize, one of the highest honors an author writing in Spanish can receive.

Montejo's work reflects, above all, the end of agrarian life in a particular place in the world and the emotional shifts accompanying such a bewildering change. He frequently muses on the subject of time, on loss as presence, on the immutability of spirit. We also see Montejo's fascination with the act of writing poetry and with the role language plays in all things human, including eros and birth. His work ranges in genre and tone—

appearing at times deceptively simple, strangely familiar, sober, serene, quietly urgent, compassionate—yet remains distinctive and unified from his first book to his last. "His voice, his counsel, his goodwill," Antonio López Ortega observes, "impress us in any and all circumstances, softening even the most obdurate spirit."[1] For these reasons, among others, he will be missed. His obituary in *El Universal* (Caracas) notes that Montejo was "one of those beings who enriched us greatly, since even though he is gone he left us his words. Thank God he left many, because the vacuum his death creates is immense."[2]

Montejo's first book, *Human Paradise,* a collection of sonnets, appeared in 1959, while he was completing a law degree at the University of Carabobo. Metrically precise, highly stylized and literary, the poems mainly explore the subject of love.[3] Although Montejo excluded this early (and now unavailable) work from his corpus, it is worth remarking on, as it will figure in his later work, most prominently in *The Silk Axe* (1995), a pseudonymous book of sonnets constructed in high classical tradition. *Human Paradise* also stands as a reaction against the late-modern surrealist poetics popularized and epitomized by Pablo Neruda and Octavio Paz, and against the straightforwardly political poetry in vogue in the 1950s. While Montejo's official first book, *Elegies,* published in 1967, does, in its way, bow to late modern trends (experimental grammar, poems without titles), the clarity and serenity of this book and each book that follows are striking, considering the artistic climate. Compared with poems by others writing in Latin America in the 1960s and 1970s, Montejo's seem bare and unadorned. Instead of obscurity and surreal disjunction, we find elegant simplicity, often in outwardly plain language. As Francisco José Cruz Pérez observes, the poems "flow out untrammeled, in precise, everyday language, language all but free of experimentalism, but full of experience."[4] In a preface to a recent reprinting of *A Few Words,* Montejo noted that he had hoped to distance himself from "the modernist experimentation saturating the first half of our century," seeking words that might bring him "nearer to the speech of our people and our countryside."[5] His art is conspicuously apolitical; unlike Ernesto Cardenal, Roque Dalton, Fayad Jamis, or Heberto Padilla—to name just a few of the politically engaged—Montejo chose not to engage, at least not directly. Instead of vitriol directed at governments, we find transcendent images, birds singing in trees in forests razed years before.

With the burgeoning of an international oil industry in Venezuela in the 1940s and 1950s, along with accelerated mining and the building of dams, Montejo witnessed in his youth not just unprecedented economic growth but also massive environmental devastation. The Venezuela he knew as a child, an agrarian, often densely forested landscape, became a noisy, polluted, heavily populated, cosmopolitan sprawl almost overnight. His poetry, particularly the poems he wrote in the 1970s and 1980s, reflects all of this. In Montejo's poetic tableaux, writes María Alejandra Gutiérrez, trees are "palpable beings," and the ghost music of disappeared birds from vanished forests continues unchanged, while stones in their silence offer instruction about permanence in our ephemeral earthly existence.[6] The poems are very much occupied by the past and by memory, but never in ways that seem nostalgic. Montejo's "resurrection of the past," as Miguel Gomes notes, "never freezes the present."[7] The work invokes what is lost or gone or dead—wilderness, friends, loved ones, states of mind, situations— not by clinging to but by embodying that past to make change and death seem less final, evoking realms where past, present, and future coexist. Poem by poem, as Cruz Pérez suggests, we find that "time is a lesson we have not yet learned." To remember, in this sense, is to create a meeting place where times reunite, with memory occupying a kind of "time before time."[8] What we experience line by line, finally, is an earthbound but not earth-heavy transcendence, a yearning equanimity, detached but not distant, visionary without ever seeming explicitly so.

If *Elegies* is a book exploring memory and death, Montejo's second book, *Death and Memory* (1972), extends the meditation more explicitly and straightforwardly. In his third book, *A Few Words* (1976), these subjects merge with concerns about the natural world and humankind's place in it. "In the time that remains," Montejo writes in a poem of the same name, "let's teach stones to speak. / A little patience will do, a little snow, / a less guarded sobbing." The poem ends quietly, if post-apocalyptically: "They'll be able to tell all alone / the earth's final tale, / recall us at the ocean's edge / when waves drag other slow logs along." In *Terredad* (1978), Montejo's fourth and most anthologized volume, earth and transcendence, along with the pervasive issue of time, figure foremost. This book speaks to the paradoxes of time, transience, finitude and infinity, and beyond; its serene voice of equanimity is seasoned by the wisdom of lifetimes of knowing. The neologism *"terredad"* plays on the word *"humanidad"* (humanity), suggesting much: that as sentient entities, the earth and its nonhuman creatures deserve consideration, respect, and compassion; that the earth and its humans are more connected than one might imagine; that we have not found words yet to express such interrelation (what Zen Buddhist monk Thich Nhat Hanh calls, using his own neologism, "interbeing"). Or, to cite Guillermo Sucre: "Identity, but not ownership, wisdom, but not knowledge: *terredad* can accommodate material and immaterial, concrete and virtual. Above all it is a rhythm, a dynamism in which all life participates, memory especially."[9]

Terredad's first poem ponders the place of humankind in the woods; its last is an eerie, breezy monologue by a tree. *Terredad* is thus "in large part a book about trees and birds," Américo Ferrari points out, "which is to say an attempt on the poet's part to write (fulfilling the promises one finds in certain poems in *A Few Words*)—to inscribe in the weave of the poem, since every poem is an inscription—the voice of the wind murmuring indistinctly in branches and leaves, or of birdsong."[10] The book's title poem employs such a voice, and the perspective it offers is simultaneously terrestrial, transcendental, and cosmological:

> To be here these years on earth
> with clouds moving in, birds
> suspended in the delicate hours.
> On board and all but adrift,
> nearer to Saturn and then farther off,
> while the sun spins and drags us along
> and the blood runs its infinitesimal cosmos,
> holier even than the stars.

Strikingly, the birds here are "suspended" in a literal way, floating on updrafts of wind, even as they are held aloft by time's liquidity, by memory, and by the poem itself, with "birds" hovering at the end of the line to fully embody suspension. "On board and all but adrift," all planetary sojourners are likewise suspended—in this case by the dance of celestial bodies, a process occurring both inward and out, on levels cosmologically macro and micro. Fittingly, Montejo has been described as a "cosmic poet," one whose "cosmovision" tends toward new modes of perceiving, toward openings into new ontological realms and dimensions.[11] By avoiding or de-centering the poetic "I," Montejo's poems offer a "new cosmic order," as

Gomes suggests—an order "more just and less oriented by hierarchies. It is a cosmology in which nothing is central—and nothing is peripheral."[12] Poem by poem, time and other human conceptions are gently dismantled, subsumed, or exposed as the frail scaffolds they indeed seem to be. "In Montejo's poems," Cruz Pérez observes, "rather than seeing how the days pass, we feel the earth turning."[13]

Absolute Tropics (1982), a sequel of sorts to Terredad, is a series of poems extending and particularizing the earlier book, affording a sharper poetic landscape, a more clearly defined Venezuela. The work echoes Vicente Gerbasi, Pablo Neruda, Jules Supervielle, and Walt Whitman; the lyricism of certain poems seems an effort to reincorporate the poetic "I" within a pantheistic, omnisciently de-centered perspective. "If I return again," Montejo writes in a poem, "it will be / because of the singing of birds." His speaker continues: "I may not hear a thing in the vacuum / but my voice will rise by the choirs nonetheless." Montejo's sixth book of poetry, Alphabet of the World (1986), selects from and anthologizes the earlier volumes of verse while offering thirty-seven new poems to the mix. As its title suggests, a number of the new poems are about the act of writing itself. Significantly, some of the early poems (most noticeably those from Elegies) reappear in substantially revised form. Montejo's concern with the problem of writing, tangential in the earlier "Letra Profunda," and "The Trees," for instance, now becomes central in "Letters" and "Writing" and "Alphabet of the World," among other poems. Still, Montejo's writing about writing seems distinctly unrelated to what one tends to call "postmodernism." The verse is free of suspicion and gleeful despair, of self-effacing jouissance and writerly solipsism, and never parades the fact of its own virtuosity; poetry like Montejo's tends rather to conceal its artifice. Instead, we find sober reflection rendered in "measured intonations" (to use Guillermo Sucre's phrase), language almost entirely unwilling to traffic in irony.[14] "No pencils," we hear in "Writing"; the poem's speaker says he has "had it with words," and that, paring down, he will write someday with stones, "the elemental bareness of feeling / imprinting its deep secret music / in the hearts of rocks."

To some degree, one must suppose that the "deep secret music" is not language or music at all, but the flip side or counterpart of language and sound. If, as Sucre notes, Montejo is fascinated by language, in book after book "he is also equally fascinated by silence," and Alphabet of the World and the volumes that follow it attest to this well.[15] Among contemporary Latin American poets, "Montejo knows best how to privilege the clarity and sobriety of necessary silence," to cite Edmundo Bracho. "The form with which he compels the natural elements in his lines is an essential characteristic of his detailed, diaphanous entry into life's mystery: tree, river, bird, rooster, rooster that sings, song of *terredad*."[16] In *Farewell to the Twentieth Century* (1992, 1997), the next book of verse, Montejo delivers his most concise statement on craft with "Poetry," an *ars poetica* that delivers most where it delivers least:

> Poetry traverses the earth alone
> investing its voice in the pain of the world;
> it asks for nothing—
> > not even words.

Accordingly, as Montejo reveals in an interview, poetry is the "word visited by silence," the word itself (as he notes elsewhere) occupying "the center of being."[17] The human component of *terredad*, therefore, involves understanding and respecting the nuances of the language we speak, recognizing it each hour of each day as the vital instrument it is. Thus does poetry arrive without warning at whatever hour—as Montejo describes it in "Poetry"—letting itself in at the door ("it's got the key") and pausing to study us. "Later," we read, "it opens its hand and delivers / a flower, or pebble, something secret / but so intense the heart beats / too quickly. And we awaken."

Montejo suggests that the apprenticeship of a poet is long and fraught with mystery, and that what one learns is not necessarily concrete, or conclusive. He notes of learning his craft, "it was indispensable to manage on my own the alphabet and its infinite combinations. The alphabet of the world, whose symbols we know well but cannot fully decipher in the course of a life."[18] The deciphering continues in the most recent volumes of verse: *The Cicada's Score* (1999), *Love Parchments* (2002, 2003), and *The Scribe's Fable* (2006). The poems themselves are more expansive (longer poems, here and there; some multi-segmented, divided in cantos, or in the case of the last book, "pavanes"), and many venture into new subject matter (every poem in *Love Parchments* is indeed a love poem). Montejo writes in "Written in Passing" (from *The Cicada's Score*) that the poet "doesn't sing, it would be useless / he dodges dimness and madness / without uttering a word."

And yet "In this long night / his voice is lightning / that is creating heat elsewhere." In a poem from *The Scribe's Fable*—one utilizing the old cosmovision, but singing about singing with even greater compression—Montejo's speaker gazes upon "the blue wheel of cosmos," and, reflecting on time and belief, concludes: "The song from out there / comes from so far it hardly fits / the small feathered body. / And yet at this hour / if something's left of God / we hear it in birds."

Montejo's heteronymic works—in which he assumes characters of different fictional authors—draw from the tradition of Fernando Pessoa, Antonio Machado, Valéry Larbaud, Gottfried Benn, Roque Dalton, and others. They are essential complements to the poetry bearing his own name; they enhance his overall work by reflecting and refracting his recurrent subjects and themes. Even so, the books are intense and memorable on their own, and do much more than deepen and inform his poetic achievement. All five heteronymic books—*The Notebook of Blas Coll* (1981, 1983, 2006), *Guitar of the Horizon* (1991), *The Silk Axe* (1995), *Chamario* (2005), and *Hunting the Lightning* (2006)—derive from material Montejo claims to have discovered, salvaged, or otherwise reclaimed from obscurity. The five "authors" were at one time residents of Puerto Malo, a fictional Venezuelan fishing village, and all kept notebooks, each of which Montejo offers to the reading public with a preface written by him. Each notebook provides an alternate vehicle and guise for spelling out the alphabet of the world, for learning its language, and for furthering the act of "deciphering." These "indirect voices," as Montejo tended to call them, are not simply literary modes or devices. As Arturo Gutiérrez Plaza observes, Montejo's heteronymic forays "reflect a way of seeing reality, of seeing oneself in that reality, above all; given multiple viewpoints the poet can widen his range of vision, taking as points of departure subjects and forms he might otherwise deem contradictory to assumptions about his 'identity.'" In this sense, Montejo's "heteronymia" is not so much a technique as it is "a way of thinking and of situating oneself in the world."[19]

The Notebook of Blas Coll, the first of these texts, features the philosophical musings of an aging, eccentric printer, an autodidact who ultimately invents his own language to replace what he considers the filtering, falsifying, hypocritical, unholy enterprise of Spanish. Gradually he loses his mind, or so it would seem; he turns voluntarily mute, isolates himself, destroys nearly all of his writing, and disappears. *The Notebook of Blas Coll* is a kind of Borgesian narrative; Coll's surviving "notes" (in large part illegible or encrypted) are interpolated by editorial comments by "Eugenio Montejo," who, yearning for more pieces and clues, admits that the fragments he has assembled do not quite cohere. Coll as a literary figure seems most directly inspired by the real-life Simón Rodriguez, an uproarious and unconventional nineteenth-century Venezuelan writer and tutor (who taught Simón Bolívar), and by the fictional Juan de Mairena, a creation of Spain's Antonio Machado, the first poet to write heteronymically in Spanish. Coll's statements are epigrammatic, frenetic, at times almost heart-stoppingly beautiful. More often than not, they are terribly true—true to the point of absurdity. "The structure of speech," he insists, for example, "should vary over the course of the day, marking for us in the clearest way possible the passing of time. It is not useful to speak in the morning the way we do in the evening."

Coll and his creator have much in common; both sustain an ongoing preoccupation with language, hoping to get their alphabets right, and both try to tune in to the earth's way of speaking and to what lies beyond. "Nature is shorthand," Coll writes, in his own fledgling shorthand. He further observes: "Every clause must replicate in its construction, as closely as possible, the gravitational pull of the known stars. The subject must rotate like the sun." The old printer's radical views are not shared by Montejo, but as Cruz Pérez notes, Coll does "illuminate the plight of the poet, and further situate the ongoing dilemma concerning verbal time versus real time" and highlights especially "the lucid poverty of writing in the face of a world in motion."[20] The fact that *The Notebook of Blas Coll* underwent substantial revision in the course of its five printings and grew in these last years to more than a third larger than its original size seems to acknowledge this split, this pull between the word and the world, and to address the dilemma more fully, if not find reconciliation. As Óscar Marcano suggests, Coll "proposes a language of clarity, capable of translating all things," a language capturing "revelation and music, and generating aesthetic complexity and intimate accord. In other words, he is proposing to make poetry language."[21]

Montejo's four other heteronymic texts are drawn from notebooks purportedly penned by Blas Coll's disciples, or *colígrafos,* as Montejo calls them in his prefaces to their work. In *Guitar of the Horizon* we are introduced to Sergio Sandoval, a retiring, self-effacing, pacifist poet whose *coplas,* or anonymous stanzas, embody popular folk tradition even as they incorporate and engage Eastern thought—Taoism and Zen in particular. (The *copla*—simultaneously complex and simple—has been around since the beginning in Spanish literature, tied as it is to folk tradition and agrarian song; Venezuelan poet Alfredo Arvelo Larriva is particularly known today for the form, as is popular Venezuelan singer Simón Díaz.) Each of the fifty *coplas* in *Guitar of the Horizon* is followed by a short piece by Sandoval, a kind of interpretive gloss in prose whose resonance rivals that of the poem itself. The book's seventh *copla* presents a bird singing in a palm tree, singing and singing as the tree is battered by wind. Sandoval observes in his gloss:

> Hard as the wind blows, the palm fronds are trained to withstand; they make use of the onslaught, shaking unresistingly at the wind's whim. As gusts tear at the branches the crown sways; the bird's feathers all stand on end. Only its song stays unchanged, and though its melody repeats endlessly it's still always new, tapping a root deeper than that of any tree on earth.

Sandoval's measured voice is a far cry from Coll's, but similar in mission and impact. If Sandoval is "a mystic who reclaims for the popular *copla* the same spiritual dignity of haiku," as Montejo states in an interview, he is a particularly palatable one; it is a reclamation that persona and poet effect seemingly effortlessly, one underlining Montejo's themes yet again: transience and transcendence, music that surpasses mortality.[22] The song persists, despite all calamity—transmitted from tree to *copla* to gloss to reader to new generations of readers, and farther. The bird's song and poet's song persevere, deeply connected to that which binds all: to *terredad,* one assumes, no matter how weightless or finite the vessel.

The final three heteronymic books (not anthologized here) offer other uniquely "indirect voices" that further color and complicate Montejo's corpus. *The Silk Axe* comprises sonnets by one Tomás Linden, half Swedish and half Venezuelan, who as an adult returns to Venezuela, the land of his birth. In his role as one of Blas Coll's *colígrafos,* he moves gracefully into something approaching strict classical form, daring to risk sentimentality without falling into sentimentality's traps. *Chamario* is a book of rhymes written for children by Eduardo Polo, called "the magician of Puerto Malo," thanks to the spellbinding effects he achieves in his poems. It is the only text by a *calígrafo* allegedly published by Coll, and it is the only surviving work by Polo, who, it is said, destroyed all his work before moving away and dedicating himself to music and marine biology in another Caribbean country. The last of the heteronymic texts, *Hunting the Lightning,* by Lino Cervantes ("Puerto Malo's Percival," as he was called), is a book of poetic "coligrams" tapping the experimental techniques of Guillaume Apollinaire and Vicente Huidobro. This book is perhaps the closest any of the *calígrafos* have come to realizing Coll's credos in written form. As Montejo explains in the book's preface, the term "hunting the lightning" approximates aptly enough "the sense of [Lino] Cervantes's lyrical pursuit"; one's longing to hunt in this way "seems to translate the secret wish to reach light that a word imparts before being converting to pure silence."[23] Each poem by Cervantes is funnel-shaped, traveling down the page in a gradually narrowing taper, its language compressing and collapsing line by line, rarifying to essential consonants and vowels:

> Y para mis palabras los ojos de las piedras
> Y pris pabras lojis pedras
> Pabris liperdes
> Pribas lópedras
> Prílobi
> Proi

Only the first lines of these poems appear in Spanish; this poem, titled simply "XXIX," begins, "And for my words the eyes of stones." Line by line, we hear human language gradually fuse with the voice of the wind, or the river, or with the chirps and whirrs of cicadas and birds. Or, in this case, perhaps we hear murmurs from stones: those that tell the earth's final tale after human seeing and singing end—after transmigration occurs and poets inhabit stones fully.

Nor, it seems, is Puerto Malo about to stop speaking. Other figures linger in its mists, distinct persons and personalities, friends of Blas Coll, if not *calígrafos*; had Montejo lived longer, more texts might have surfaced. A shadowy figure, Jorge Silvestre, lurks at the fringe; Montejo dedicates poems to him in *The Cicada's Score* and *Love Parchments.* Silvestre is the purported author of a blurb for *Hunting the Lightning* (as are

Sergio Sandoval, Tomás Linden, Eduardo Polo, and others) in which he recalls hearing Cervantes's voice reading verse on cassette, sounding like "a completely foreign language" whose tones he nonetheless seems to have "heard in some other life." There is Felipe Terrán, millionaire patron (fattened during the reign of the dictator Marcos Pérez Jiménez) of the *colígrafos*, who spent most days on his yacht with a professor of Latin, transporting one poet or another to one place or another. There is also Diego Álvarez, who played chess with the group and participated in their high-minded discussions; he is unique (and proud of the fact) in being the only non-writer among the coterie. He is also the only member still living. And since no one ever offered to put the group's story on paper, Álvarez has (perhaps to his own embarrassment and discredit) begun a novel, apparently connecting the *colígrafos*' lives. Montejo had found the draft, naturally. Which begins: "I don't know if this is any way to start, or where such a beginning might lead, but reading and writing are what I hate most in life."[24]

Through his heteronymic cast, Montejo not only sees from multiple angles, but also—text after text and text *within* text—cultivates multiple selves. He explains in an interview that his effort to recreate "an homage to the Golden Age" through the guise of the fictional Tomás Linden constitutes "an attempt to explore those other sides of [himself]. Not unlike what Cubism did for Machado, Pessoa, and Gottfried Benn when they were beginning to write. Which is to say to look at an object not just from the frontal, uniquely human perspective, but also to look simultaneously from six possible views, from the six faces of the cube."[25] For Montejo, then, the assumption of names and personae is not so much an act of creating masks as it is its opposite. As Gutiérrez Plaza suggests, Montejo's indirect voices "emerge as reflections of an expressive need that paradoxically reveal multiple views."[26]

It is not surprising to learn, therefore, that "Eugenio Montejo" is itself an invented name. Born Eugenio Hernández Álvarez, by age twenty-one, with the publication of *Human Paradise*, he had already adopted his pen name, no doubt for its euphonious sound and its association with nature, specifically mountains.[27] Knowing that "Montejo" is a pen name further complicates already complicated issues and nuances regarding his work. The fictional author Tomás Linden, for instance, is supposedly friends with Maqroll, a fictional character created by Colombian novelist and poet

Álvaro Mutis, even as we learn of Linden partially through his mentor, Blas Coll, who is like Linden a creation of Eugenio Montejo, a Venezuelan poet who in turn has created himself.

Eugenio Hernández Álvarez was born in Caracas on October 19, 1938. His mother was raised in the capital; his father, a baker, originated in the village of Güigüe, farther north, a descendent of immigrants from the Canary Islands (where Blas Coll apparently originated). The second of ten children, Eugenio grew up in Maracay, in the state of Aragua, southwest of the capital. He attended secondary school (a military academy) in La Grita, in the state of Táchira, and completed a law degree at the University of Carabobo in Valencia, Venezuela. He also studied sociology at the Sorbonne in Paris and spent much time abroad, in Buenos Aires, London, and a handful of other European cities. By this time he had begun working for the university press and culture department of his alma mater and would work for many years after as an editor, most prominently as chief literary editor at Monte Ávila Editores, in Caracas. He served for a while as Venezuela's cultural attaché in Portugal but did not devote himself to diplomacy as other Latin American authors did (such as Venezuelan poets Fernando Paz Castillo or Vicente Gerbasi before him).

His first book was published in 1959, a year significant for a number of reasons. The Cuban Revolution took place that year. Venezuela's first popularly elected government began that year as well, signaling the end of the reign of Marcos Pérez Jiménez, one of the country's most tyrannical dictators. That year marked the beginning of what is now considered Venezuela's cultural renaissance. The first Venezuelan Theater Festival was held in 1959. The state began creating facilities and foundations for the arts, establishing prizes for artists, and founding presses. Plans for an Instituto Nacional de la Cultura y Bellas Artes were in the air, even as novelists, old and young, moved in new and striking directions, into formal experimentation and unconventional subjects and themes (José Balza, Salvador Garmendia, Adriano González León, Carlos Noguera, and Miguel Otero Silva, to name a few). Poetry visibly flourished, too. Poets constituting the Venezuelan "Generation of '58" were wide-ranging and many, even if (as one expects) male: Rafael Cadenas, Juan Calzadilla, Ramón Palomares, Francisco Pérez Perdomo, Juan Sánchez Peláez, Alberto Silva Estrada, Guillermo Sucre, and others. In the midst of all this, Eugenio Montejo arose, "at the tail end of the Generation of '58," as he put it, despite his uneasiness about being pigeonholed, or of ascribing too much in the way of affinity. He founded a literary journal, *Azar Rey,* during those days, and co-founded another, *Poesía.* He came of age with his country, artistically speaking—effloresced with its arts—but did not find himself completely tied to Caracas, or to Venezuela. He was able to travel and study in Europe because the government had lately begun offering grants to young writers and artists hoping to further their training abroad.

Most of the material Montejo later published in his books of essays—*Indirect Views* (1974) and *The White Workshop* (1983, 1996)—was written abroad and mailed back for publication in Venezuelan magazines, newspapers, and journals. Many of these essays are appraisals and explorations of poets and poetry, contemporary or otherwise. He treats Paul Valéry, Arthur Rimbaud, C.P. Cavafy, Novalis, Antonio Machado, Jules Supervielle, Giuseppe Ungaretti, Lucian Blaga, Carlos Pellicer, Luis Cernuda, and Juan Sánchez Peláez, to name a few; by focusing on the craft of other poets, he shaped his own craft and aesthetic, and revealed to a degree the dimensions of his own artistic tenets. The three essays here anthologized reflect Montejo's range as an essayist. Probing and charismatic, they shed light specifically on the poems and heteronymic work they accompany. "Fear of Falling in K" is an intriguingly humorous Blas Collian meditation on the letter "K," on language, on ontological fear, and on Kafka. "Poetry in a Time Without Poetry" addresses the permutations of the late-twentieth-century Latin American poem (its place, its roots, its directions) and dissects and examines certain truisms concerning the era. Finally, "The White Workshop," a personal essay, a kind of *ars poetica* in prose, details Montejo's formation and evolution as a writer. Montejo reflects at length, directly as well as metaphorically, on his own creative process. The essay is atypical of him in offering autobiographical glimpses of a private, highly reticent writer, who, personal as the material might seem, is not about to explain his own mysteries away.

Nor did he ever, as it turns out, on the printed page or in life. Reserved and understated till the end, he made his exit quietly, uncomplainingly, without fanfare—to the surprise and shock of many who knew him, including this volume's co-introducers. Eugenio's penultimate letter to one of us, dated November 6, 2007, is more ominous than optimistic. It reads, in part:

Dear Kirk:

Excuse me for the lateness of my reply. I was in a clinic, undergoing emergency surgery for an intestinal perforation. I am recovering, but have had a considerable scare.

Until lately I hadn't been operated on before, ever. This year I chose to have eye surgery, and now suddenly I am leveled by this grave mishap that scarcely allowed me time to tell about it. I have overcome it now, fortunately.[28]

He spent his last days at the Centro Policlínico "La Viña" in Valencia, Venezuela, near his father's hometown, and died late in the evening of June 5, 2008, of stomach cancer. In the presence of friends and family, including his second wife, Aymara Pinto, and his sons, Emilio Alvar and Ivo Ricardo, he was buried there, in Valencia—not in Caracas, his birthplace, the metropolis in which he had spent more than thirty years. Montejo was "a poet of goodbyes," novelist Juan Villoro observed in an obituary in Mexico's *Prensa Fondo.* "He bid farewell to the twentieth century, to his father, his friends, to Lisbon, and to other poets transformed to statues, including himself. Evoking what fades and returns as enduring absence was his way of being present."[29]

Surprising and not surprising, Venezuela's government failed to honor the poet according to protocol—the customary page or half-page memorial ads, notices announcing that the Ministry of Culture regrets the passing of the distinguished artist in question, and so on. Surprising, because rude lapses must always seem so; and not surprising, because, apolitical as the poetry remained till the end, Montejo's criticism of President Hugo Chávez's iron-fisted regime had toward the end become increasingly pointed, searing, and direct. He publicly decried, for example, the "veiled censorship" afflicting his country, a situation he called "less than favorable to intellectuals."[30] He regretted seeing basic human rights crumble around him, year by year, day after day; he was aggravated in particular by Chávez's gradual takeover of communications media, and by the fact that the man had tampered with, adjusted, and finally rewritten the country's constitution to make his term of office permanent. (The constitutional revision was later rejected by voters in a referendum.) Interviewed by Spain's *El País,* Montejo lamented that "Chávez violates all the rules, beginning with the meaning of words."[31] Though the poet had basked in his youth in the glow of the fall of one authoritarian ruler, he found his later years darkened, if not quite dimmed, by the rise of another. Still, Montejo was far from outspoken, in conversation or on the page. "He was a discreet man," Juan Villoro observes, a man "who chose to speak in a low voice, his education forever present but never paraded. . . . In the country of vociferous Hugo Chávez, the poet Montejo's restraint was indispensable ethical courage."[32]

Montejo's work from beginning to end is unique—serene, uncanny, unsettling, vibrant, intense—as well as courageous, and timely, and *needed,* no less, in this age of business first and fear and to-hell-with-Kyoto. The present book stands as Montejo's U.S. debut. It also reclaims in part certain of his texts for readers of Spanish who have hoped to get glimpses of his books that have been out of print for years. Not unlike his poems, his prose reminds us "how language constructs us," to cite Cruz Pérez; the essays insist in their various ways that language "is not just one of our instruments."[33] The work across genres attests to an ongoing, unending apprenticeship, at once universal and particular, in life and in letters. It embodies Montejo's commitment not solely to craft but to understanding how the world and mind work and to representing them faithfully and sincerely on the page—even when faith and sincerity enlist the support of created identities. In Montejo's poetry there are "no blind alleys or false starts, nor thunderclaps or fireworks," López Ortega writes. "Poetry of essence, tapping the core of the matter that animates us, to know ourselves as transcendent beings, and to celebrate—even in incomprehension—the miracle of being."[34] This anthology, *Alphabet of the World,* aims to render at least some of this essence, and much of its mystery. At best it is a beginning. The individual Montejo volumes will follow in time, early to late, book after book, we can be sure.

NOTES

1. Antonio López Ortega, "Entrevista a Eugenio Montejo," in *Recital* (Caracas: Espacios Unión, 1999), 5. Passage translated by Nesset, as are all of the critical citations and segments from interviews that follow. All but one of the essays, articles, and interviews cited here were written and published in Spanish; the sole essay about Montejo in English appearing to date (a book introduction) is by Miguel Gomes, below.

2. Carmen Rosa Gómez, "Montejo: El Ausente Siempre Presente," *El Universal* (Caracas), June 7, 2008, www.eluniversal.com/2008/06/07/til_art_montejo:-el-au sente_894748.shtml.

3. For purposes of interest and reference, we offer a poem in Spanish and English from *Humano paraíso* (Valencia, Venezuela: Impresiones Clima, 1959), translated by Wilfredo Hernández:

Nocturno:

¿Oís alada música de mojadas cadencias?
¿Qué tecla o ave herida gime con este grillo?
Venid, nocturnas aves de azules transparencias
y escuchad de cristal persistente estribillo!
¿Por quién toca? ¡Venid, hormigas rojas
y azulejos insomnes, venid a este concierto
donde un grillo o cristal de melodiosas hojas
preludia solitario por lo vivo y lo muerto!
¿No escucháis diminuta posesión de murmullos,
casi roce de manos desnudas, poseyéndose,
bajo una luz al vuelo de instantáneos cocuyos?
—Os aguarda la noche misteriosa extinguiéndose,
por vosotros que abrís un ultimo capullo
para un grillo que toca su pífano riéndose . . .

Nocturne

Do you hear winged music, those watery cadences?
Which air or damaged bird laments with this cricket?
Come, nocturnal birds of transparent blue,
hear the persistent crystal refrain!
For whom do they play? Come, red ants
and sleepless blue tanagers, come to this concert
where a cricket or a crystal of melodious leaves
rehearses alone for the living and dead!
Can you not hear little currents of murmurs,
like the graze of naked hands entwined in love
under the sporadic glow of lightning bugs?
The waning night mysteriously awaits you,
you who unfold one last bud
for a cricket playing its fife, laughing . . .

4. Francisco José Cruz Pérez, "Eugenio Montejo: El viaje total," in *Antología*, by Eugenio Montejo (Caracas: Monte Ávila Editores, 1996), 25.

5. Eugenio Montejo, prologue to the 2nd ed. of *Algunas palabras* (Maracay, Venezuela: La Liebre Libre, 1995), 5.

6. María Alejandra Gutiérrez, "El diálogo con el enigma de Eugenio Montejo," *Literaturas: Revista Literaria Independiente de los Nuevos Tiempos* (Spain, 2002), www.literaturas.com/EMontejoLC.htm.

7. Miguel Gomes, "Eugenio Montejo's Earthdom," in *The Trees: Selected Poems 1967–2004*, by Eugenio Montejo, trans. Peter Boyle (Cambridge, U.K.: Salt Publishing, 2004), xviii.

8. Cruz Pérez, "Eugenio Montejo," 11.

9. Guillermo Sucre, *La máscara, la transparencia* (Mexico City: Fondo de Cultura Económica, 1985), 311.

10. Américo Ferrari, "Eugenio Montejo y el alfabeto del mundo," in *Alfabeto del mundo*, by Eugenio Montejo (Barcelona: Editorial Laia, 1986), 18.

11. Francisco Rivera, "La poesía de Eugenio Montejo," *Inscripciones* (Caracas: Fundarte, 1982).[I added this FN; needs to be verified by Kirk Nesset and page number added if he has it.—KF]

12. Gomes, "Eugenio Montejo's Earthdom," xx.

13. Cruz Pérez, "Eugenio Montejo," 15.

14. Sucre, *Máscara*, 312.

15. Ibid.

16. Edmundo Bracho, "Respuestas para Edmundo Bracho," in *Geometría de las horas*, by Eugenio Montejo (Veracruz: Universidad Veracruzana, 2006), 357.

17. Montejo, "Textos para una meditación sobre lo poético," *Zona Franca* (Caracas) ser. 3, no. 39 (1966), 20; Montejo, interviewed in Gutiérrez, "Diálogo," 5.

18. Montejo, "Al recibir el premio Octavio Paz," in *Geometría de las horas*, 300.

19. Arturo Gutiérrez Plaza, "El alfabeto de la terredad: Estudio de la poética en la obra de Eugenio Montejo," *Revista Iberoamericana* 60, no. 166–67 (1994): 560.

20. Cruz Pérez, "Eugenio Montejo," 21.

21. Óscar Marcano, "Veinticinco años de *El cuaderno de Blas Coll*," *Papel Literario*, supplement to *El Nacional* (Caracas), August 5, 2006: 3.

22. Eugenio Montejo, interviewed by Francisco José Cruz Pérez, "Entrevista a Eugenio Montejo," in *Geometría de las horas*, by Eugenio Montejo, 375.

23. Montejo, preface to *La caza del relámpago*, in *El cuaderno de Blas Coll seguido de La caza del rela_mpago por Lino Cervantes* (Caracas: Bid & Co. Editor, 2006), 86.

24. We are indebted to Marcano, "Veinticinco años," for some of the information here regarding the other members of Coll's circle, which he gleaned from conversations and correspondence with Montejo.

25. Montejo, interviewed by López Ortega, "Entrevista," 13.

26. Gutiérrez Plaza, "Alfabeto," 560.

27. Creating a pen name had by this time in twentieth-century Latin America become a fairly old-fashioned thing for poets to do. Nicaragua's late-nineteenth-century poet Rubén Darío adopted his pen name, as did Pablo Neruda early in the twentieth century. The poets of Montejo's generation for the most part did not.

28. Montejo, e-mail to Kirk Nesset, November 6, 2007. The text of the letter in Spanish reads as follows:

Querido Kirk:

Excúsame por el retardo de mi respuesta. Estuve en una clínica, intervenido de emergencia a causa de una perforación intestinal. Ya me voy reponiendo, pero he pasado un susto considerable.

Nunca antes había sido operado. Este año decidí la operación de los ojos y ahora, de súbito, me sobrevino este grave percance que casi no me da tiempo para contarlo. Afortunadamente ya lo he superado.

29. Juan Villoro, "El pan dormido," *Prensa Fondo,* June 28, 2008, www.fondo deculturaeconomica.com/prensaDetalle.asp?art=16764, reprinted from *Reforma* (Mexico City), June 13, 2008.

30. "Falleció el poeta Eugenio Montejo," *Letralia* (Caguas, Venezuela), June 6, 2008, www.letralia.com/188/0605montejo.htm.

31. Montejo, interviewed by Javier Rodríguez Marcos, "Chávez viola el significado de las palabras," *El País* (Madrid), February 14, 2008, www.elpais.com/articulo/ultima/C%20havez/viola/significado/palabras/elpepucul/20080214elpepiult_2/Tes. On this particular matter, Montejo was very direct, too, by way of personal correspondence. In an e-mail to Nesset dated May 30, 2007, for example, he wrote:

En tu carta pasada me preguntabas por qué Chávez tiene tanta gente que lo apoya aún. No creo que sea tanta, pero son muy astutos en propaganda. En esto, como en todo, el gobierno está asesorado por los cubanos, que son expertos en propaganda. Todos los poderes están bajo el absoluto control de Chávez, y entre ellos el electoral, de modo que es imposible ganarle ninguna elección. En el Parlamento no hay un diputado de oposición, pues se negaron a asistir a las votaciones en protesta por el sistema electoral. Sin embargo, pese a que todos los diputados son de su partido, Chávez pidió poderes especiales para gobernar por decreto y modificar la Constitución—la misma que ellos aprobaron hace pocos años— pues ahora desea incluir entre los artículos la reelección vitalicia.

En la actualidad tiene muchas televisoras y radios que controla, pero no le basta pues no quiere ninguna opinión contraria. Por ahora queda una sola televisión que da opinión distinta, y ayer mismo en su comunicación al país la amenazó con cerrarla.

La protesta por el cierre, sin embargo, ha sido condenada por muchas organizaciones y medios. Periódicos tan serios como *Le Monde, The Guardian, El País, ABC,* etc., la han condenado. Asimismo la Unión Europea, el Congreso de USA, y casi todos los diarios y gobiernos hispanoamericanos. El problema de Chávez es que confunde una verdad con una idea fija.

32. Villoro, "Pan dormido."

33. Cruz Pérez, "Entrevista," 378.

34. López Ortega, "Liminar," preface to 2nd ed. of *Papiros amorosos,* by Eugenio Montejo (Caracas, Fundación Bigott, 2003), 5.

Poems

From *Élegos* (1967)

Mayo

al Dr. José Solanes

Mayo nos abre su día blanco
en la llovizna de amanecida,
azota el viento los terrados
con su furia gélida y el agua
se arrebuja en la piedad de los bajantes.

Es mayo aún su cielo plúmbeo;
gordas moscas husmean viejas cáscaras,
brotan escarabajos de la tierra húmeda
y los árboles majestuosos,
estremecidos en sus follajes oscuros,
soportan los fragores de los truenos
como quien oye graznar sus aves familiares.

From *Elegies* (1967)

May

for Dr. José Solanes

May opens its white day for us
in the drizzle of dawn;
the wind beats the roof
in its chilly fury, the water
swaddled by merciful downspouts.

It's May, despite this leaden sky;
fat flies pick at old rinds,
beetles rise from the humid earth
and magisterial trees,
trembling in dark clumps,
endure the clamor of thunder
as if hearing familiar chatter of birds.

Elegía a la muerte de mi hermano Ricardo

Mi hermano ha muerto, sus huesos yacen
caídos en el polvo. Sin ojos con qué llorar,
me habla triste, se sienta en su muerte
y me abraza con su llanto sepultado.

Mi hermano, el Rey Ricardo, murió una mañana
en un hospital de ciudad, víctima
de su corazón que trajo a la vida
fatales dolencias de familia.

Mi madre estuvo una semana muerta junto a él
y regresó con sus ojos apaleados
para mirarme de frente. Aún hay tierra
y llanto de Ricardo en sus ojos.

Perdía voz —dijo mi hermana, tenía febricitancia
de elegido y nos miraba con tanta compasión
que lloramos hasta su última madrugada.
Mamá es más pobre ahora, mucho más pobre.

Mi familia lo cercó. Él nos amaba
con la nariz taponada de algodones.
Todos éramos piedras y mirábamos
un río que comenzaba a pasar.

Lo llevaron alzado como un ave de augurios
y lo sembraron en la tierra amorosa
donde la muerte cuida a los jóvenes.
Cuando bajó, sollozaba profundo.

El Rey Ricardo está muerto. Sus pasos
de oro amargo resuenan en mi sangre
donde caminan con fragor de tormenta.
Su nombre estalla en mi boca como la luz.

Todos lo amamos, mi madre más que todos,
y en su vientre nos reunimos en un llanto compacto;
desde allí conversamos, como las piedras,
con un río que comienza a pasar.

Elegy on the Death of My Brother Richard

My brother is dead, his bones lie
strewn in the dust. With no eyes to cry,
he addresses me sadly, settled in death,
his buried weeping embracing me.

My brother King Richard died one morning
in a hospital in the city, victim
of a heart that carried in life
fatal sorrows of family.

My mother lay beside him dead a week
then returned with battered eyes
to face me directly. There's earth still
and Richard's lament in her eyes.

He lost his voice, my sister said—he had the fever
of the chosen, gazing with such compassion
we cried till the final dawn.
Mother is poorer now, much poorer.

My family encircled him. He loved us,
his nose jammed with cotton.
We were all stones, watching
a river beginning to flow.

They carried him high as a prophetic bird
and planted him in the loving earth
where death watches over the young.
The sobbing was deep as he was buried.

King Richard is dead. His steps,
bitter gold, resound in my blood,
rising like a clamoring storm.
His name in my mouth explodes like light.

We loved him, my mother most of all,
and in her womb we rejoin in a solid wail;
and there we converse, like stones,
with a river beginning to flow.

En los bosques de mi antigua casa

En los bosques de mi antigua casa
oigo el jazz de los muertos.
Arde en las pailas ese momento de café
donde todo se muda. Oréanse ropas
en las cuerdas de los góticos árboles.
Cae luz entre las piedras y se dobla
la sombra de mi vida en un reposo táctil.
Atisbo en la mudez del establo
la brida que lleve por la senda infalible.
Palpo la montura de ser y prosigo.
Cuando recorra todo llamaré ya sin nadie.
Los muertos andan bajo tierra a caballo.

In Forests of My Ancient Home

In forests of my ancient home
I hear the dead playing jazz.
Time smokes like coffee in vats
as everything turns. Clothes dry
on vines in the lugubrious trees.
Light falls on stones, folding
my life's shadow in tactile repose.
In the silence of the stable I see
the bridle worn on the infallible path.
I feel the saddle of being, proceed.
When the journey's done I will cry out unheard.
The dead pass underground on their steeds.

Mi padre regresa y duerme

Mi padre regresa y duerme;
se halla en ese límite de blanco
y de negro que me levanta
y me hunde. Me palpa
con su mano en el sueño. Se quita
su ser y su no ser, se cae
sobre sus restos hacinados
que respiran. Sabe lo que fui,
lo que seré (lo olvida al despertar).
Sus ojos hundidos yacen
en el pozo profundo
donde he sido procreado.
Mi padre regresará para nombrarme,
ahora duerme lejano; sus pies
desnudos se detienen
soñándome las leguas del camino
que habré de recorrer.

My Father Returns and Sleeps

My father returns and sleeps;
he appears in that border of white
and black that raises
and sinks me. He taps me
with his hand in the dream. He sheds himself
of being and not being, settles
into his sighing scattered
remains. He knows what I was,
what I will be (he'll forget upon waking).
His sunken eyes peer
from the deep abyss
where I was conceived.
My father will return to name me,
but sleeps now far away; his naked
feet pause for me,
dreaming the miles of highway
I will have to traverse.

Tosen viejos los árboles de invierno

Tosen viejos los árboles de invierno
sobre los blancos pavorreales de la muerte
donde la lluvia habla latín
tosen a la ululante ceniza trágica
atan valijas de partir se anochecen
y erizan los pulmones de frío
a la escarcha del rayo
ocultando ataúdes en sus capas de reyes.

Winter Trees Cough like Old Men

Winter trees cough like old men
about death's white peacocks
while the rain talks in Latin.
They cough about the sobbing tragic ash,
they bind valises for leaving, they darken—
and in the chill of frost
from the sun the lungs bristle to see
coffins hidden in the capes of kings.

From *Muerte y memoria* (1972)

Hamlet acto primero

Mira la sala: no es el cortinado
lo que tiembla. Ni la sombra de Hamlet.
Tal vez, tal vez la capa de su padre.
Todas las noches son de Dinamarca.

Los soldados se turnan en la ronda
y lían sus cigarros.
Vuelve tan crudo allí el invierno
que desdibuja en bultos blancos
la tenue imagen del televisor.
Pero la noche tiembla
y las túmidas narices del caballo
nos olfatean bajo la nieve . . .

¿Qué país no ha escondido algún Rey muerto?
Pasan las propagandas
y retornan los pasos del espectro.

Es él, es él, es su fantasma
y la venganza de esa capa sola
estremece los clavos del perchero.
El locutor anuncia otra nevada
para mañana, pero roja, siniestra.
Todas las noches son de Dinamarca.

From *Death and Memory* (1972)

Hamlet, Act One

Look in the parlor: it's not the curtain
Perhaps, just perhaps it's his father's cloak.
All nights are nights in Denmark.

Soldiers take turns on patrol
and roll cigarettes.
So raw winter is when it comes
the pale TV blurs with white streaks.
And yet the night trembles;
the horse's livid nostrils
pick us out in the snow . . .

Hasn't every country concealed a dead king?
And the propaganda flows,
the ghost's footsteps resound.

It's him, him, it's the ghost,
and for that lonely cloak revenge
rattles hooks on the coat rack.
The newscaster predicts more snow
tomorrow—red snow, sinister.
All nights are nights in Denmark.

Lejano

Noche sin gallos, sin un solo gallo
que con su grito del último ángel
nos devuelva a la casa.
Noche donde la ausencia sopla una bujía
y a oscuras oímos en el patio
a otros muertos que hablan otra lengua
y no nos acompañan.
Noche en que el río de nuestra aldea
suena ya lejos, más lejos que los astros.

Distant

Night without roosters, without a single rooster
howling like the last angel
to usher us home.
Night in which absence blows out the candle;
in the dark we hear others of the dead
on the patio who speak another tongue
and do not escort us.
Night in which our village's river
distantly flutters, farther off than the stars.

Despertar

La luz derrumba los castillos
donde flotábamos en sueño;
queda su tufarada de ballena
en nuestro espejo opaco . . .
Ya erramos cerca de Saturno,
ahora la tierra gira más despacio.
Temblamos solos en el medio del mundo
y abrimos la ventana
para que el día pase en su barco.
Anoche nos dormimos en un país tan lejano.

Waking Up

Light topples the castles
as we lie floating in dream;
its smell of rotten whale persists
in our nebulous mirror . . .
We'd been wandering along around Saturn;
the earth turns now more slowly.
We tremble alone at the world's middle
and open the window
so day might move through on its boat.
We slept last night in a world far away.

Otra lluvia

Deja que llueva sobre los terrados,
no será nunca como antaño.
Recubre entre los párpados
los planos grises del agua que cae,
verás cómo se moja tu camisa de niño.
Siempre sobre la mente quedan charcas
y nunca es fácil atravesarlas
sin regresar con los zapatos anegados.

Quienes a nuestra vuelta hacían café
y nos secaban, tienen a esta hora
la lluvia vertical entre los ojos.
Por los tejados baja a los canales
un tiempo envuelto en verdes goterones
pero no rueda lo que imaginamos.
Afuera, entre la gárgola,
llega la voz de lo que nadie sabe.

Another Rain

Let it rain on the terrace,
it'll never be like before.
Let the gray sheets descend
and glaze your eyelids,
soak the shirt you wore as a child.
Puddles always remain in the mind,
crossing over is hard
without soiling your shoes.

They who made coffee and dried us
when we came in, their eyes
hold the flood of rain now.
Days dressed in green stains
flow in spouts from the roof
but nothing we expected appears.
Outside in the uproar
a voice comes no one comprehends.

Un año

Vuelvo a contarme aquí mi vida
otra tarde de otoño,
viejo de treinta y tres vueltas al sol.
Vuelvo a replegarme en esta silla
palpando su inocencia de madera,
ahora que el año hace su estruendo
y me sacude fuerte, de raíz.
En la terraza inicio otro descenso
al infierno, al invierno.
Sangran en mí las hojas de los árboles.

A Year

I tally my life here again
on another fall afternoon,
old after thirty-three orbits of the sun.
I retreat again in this chair,
tapping its wooden innocence
as the year thunders in
and shakes me completely.
On the porch I descend again
into hell, into winter.
Leaves on trees are bleeding in me.

Salida

Seré un cadáver fácil de llevar
a través de los bosques y los mares;
en una carroza, en un blanco navío,
con lamento de corno o de fagot,
al monótono croar de los sapos . . .

Seré un cadáver inocente,
contemplativo inmóvil de mis restos,
aunque a pesar mío suene a réquiem
aquel llanto de sombra sin nadie
en los cascos del viejo caballo.

Seré un cadáver como ahora lo soy,
cavilador, absorto en lo sagrado,
pero liviano y fácil de llevar:
en una carroza, en un blanco navío,
con lamento de corno o de fagot,
al monótono croar de los sapos . . .

Exit

I'll be an easy cadaver to carry
through woods and over the sea;
in a carriage, on a white ship,
as the oboe laments, or bassoon,
over the droning croaking of toads . . .

I'll be an innocent cadaver,
quietly regarding my remains
while despite me a requiem sounds,
the moan of a lonely ghost
in the hooves of the old horse.

I'll be the cadaver I am now,
ponderous, engrossed in the holy,
though light and easy to carry:
in a carriage, on a white ship,
as the oboe laments, or bassoon,
over the droning croaking of toads . . .

From *Algunas palabras* (1976)

Sala de parto

Las madres están sentadas en hileras
junto a los muros
y el viento las disuelve.
Se oyen sus corazones apagados
y sus ojos mirándonos dispersos
desde todas las piedras.

Lo maternal torna el espacio de esta sala
en un profundo vientre;
abulta las ventanas y los cuadros,
dilata las maderas,
nos entumece con máscaras de fetos.

Finjo leer mientras aguardo a una que traje,
pero no puedo.
Los llantos de novicias, las que vienen
tarde en las ambulancias, las expertas
que añaden sus consuelos,
me repliegan en un terror extraño
como si de todas yo naciera.

Lo maternal en esta sala es la materia
en su tensión terrestre.
La rueda de las sombras, el aumento
del silencio nocturno
y el dolor que da vueltas y vueltas . . .

Salgo hacia el patio a tomar aire, a reponerme,
pero no puedo.
Me rodean otros rostros más exangües
con cenizas de ojeras
que van a pocos días del parto
en sus paseos reglamentarios,
y esos niños, esos niños que bostezan
ante este mundo de paredes tan largas.

Delivery Room

The mothers are sitting in rows
along the walls
and the wind dissolves them.
We hear their muffled hearts,
see their scattered eyes watching
in every last stone.

The maternal transforms this space
to a limitless womb;
it makes windows and framed pictures bulge,
swells the floorboards,
fills us with visions of fetuses.

I pretend to read while I wait for the woman
I brought but I can not.
The cries of the novices, they who arrive
late by ambulance, the experts
who wish to console
twist me in inexplicable terror—
as if I myself had been born.

In this room the maternal is material
in its terrestrial clasp.
A circle of phantoms, the swelling
night silence
and pain spins round and round . . .

I head for the porch to get air to revive
but cannot.
New faces encircle me, drained,
eyes ringed with ash,
faces of those who walk
the prescribed walks days after delivery,
and the babies, babies who yawn
at this world of high walls.

Letra profunda

Lo que escribí en el vientre de mi madre
ante la luz desaparece.
El sueño de mi letra antigua
tatuado en espera del mundo
se borró a la crecida del tiempo.
Colores, tactos, huellas
cayeron bajo túmulos de nieve.
Sólo murmullos a deshora
afloran hoy del fondo,
visiones en eclipse, indescifrables
que envuelve el vaho de los espejos.

Mis ojos buscan en el aire
el espacio del alma en que flotaban
y se pierden detrás de su senda.
Lo que escribí en el vientre de mi madre
quizá no fue sino una flor
porque más hiere cuando desvanece.
Una flor viva que no tiene recuerdo.

Letra Profunda

What I wrote in my mother's womb
fades before the light.
The dream of that early poem
imprinted as I awaited the world
dissolved as time flooded in.
Sensations, tints, footprints
settled under tombs of snow.
Only murmurs at odd hours
surface now from the depths,
visions eclipsed, unreadable
as steam shrouding the mirror.

My eyes seek in air
the space of soul where they hovered
and stray in its wake.
What I wrote in my mother's womb
wasn't more than a flower, perhaps—
it wounds, too, when it fades.
A living flower: no memory at all.

El otro

Miro el hombre que soy y que vuelve;
he leído en Heródoto su vida;
me habla arameo, sánscrito, sueco.

Es miope, tardo, subjetivo;
yerra por calles que declinan
hasta que el horizonte lo disuelve.

Conozco sus muertes en el Bósforo,
sus túmulos en Creta,
los sollozos en un portal oscuro
por una mujer muerta en la peste.

Llama a todas las casas de la tierra;
cambia dolor por compañía,
hastío por inocencia,
y de noche se acerca a mi lámpara
a escribir para que las nubes amanezcan
más al centro del patio,
más cerca del país que nos espera.

The Other

I see the man I am and the man who returns;
I've read his life in Herodotus;
he speaks Aramaic, Sanskrit, Swedish.

He's nearsighted, dense, highly internal;
he wanders streets that descend
till the horizon dissolves him.

I know his deaths in the Bosporus,
the great tombs on Crete,
his sobs in a dim stoop
for a woman dead from the plague.

He visits every last house on earth;
he trades pain for camaraderie,
irritation for innocence,
and nightly approaches my lamp
with his pen, so the clouds dawn
nearer my patio's center,
nearer the world that awaits.

El último pájaro

El último pájaro que canta
antes que el bosque se anochezca,
no tiene recuerdo ni esperanza,
no canta para sí, jamás se nombra,
no se refiere a nada.
Quizás en esa hora ya no es pájaro.

A la detonación oscura
con que el árbol se borra del patio
añade un grito seco,
un vidrio tenso con que cae
y se parte.

The Last Bird

The last bird that sings
before the forest dims
has neither memory nor hope;
it doesn't sing for itself, or mention itself,
or make reference to anything.
At that hour perhaps it's no longer a bird.

To the grim explosion
as the tree is erased from the patio
it adds a dry shriek,
like thin glass falling
and breaking.

Por el tiempo que quede

Por el tiempo que quede
enseñemos a hablar a las piedras.
Un poco de paciencia basta, un poco de nieve,
algún sollozo menos refractario.
Azules son las voces del Atlántico
y con rumor de caracolas ebrias,
¿por qué nadie las dice a las piedras?
Ellas quedarán por nosotros,
ellas se lavarán en el diluvio
profundas, porosas, inocentes.
Un poco de paciencia basta, un poco de nieve,
un simple amago más fraterno.
Ellas podrán contar a solas
la última historia de la tierra
y recordarnos ante el mar
cuando arrastren las olas otros leños.

In the Time That Remains

In the time that remains
let's teach stones to speak.
A little patience will do, a little snow,
a less guarded sobbing.
The voices of the Atlantic are blue,
with tipsy sea snails whispering;
why hasn't anyone told the stones?
They will remain for us,
they will bathe in the flood,
profound, porous, untainted.
A little patience will do, a little snow,
a simple sign, more humane.
They'll be able to tell all alone
the earth's final tale,
recall us at the ocean's edge
when waves drag other slow logs along.

From *Terredad* (1978)

Duración

Dura menos un hombre que una vela
pero la tierra prefiere su lumbre
para seguir el paso de los astros.
Dura menos que un árbol,
que una piedra;
se anochece ante el viento más leve,
con un soplo se apaga.
Dura menos que un pájaro,
que un pez fuera del agua;
casi no tiene tiempo de nacer;
da unas vueltas al sol y se borra
entre las sombras de las horas
hasta que sus huesos en el polvo
se mezclan con el viento.
Y sin embargo, cuando parte
siempre deja la tierra más clara.

From *Terredad* (1978)

Duration

A man lasts less long than a candle,
but the earth favors his light
to keep the stars turning.
He lasts less long than a tree,
or a stone;
he dims at the lightest breeze,
with a gust he's extinguished.
He lasts less long than a bird,
than a fish out of water;
he has almost no time to be born;
he circles the sun awhile then blots
himself out between shadows of hours
until his bones in the dust
blend with the wind.
And yet when he leaves
he always leaves the earth clearer.

Terredad

Estar aquí por años en la tierra,
con las nubes que lleguen, con los pájaros,
suspensos de horas frágiles.
A bordo, casi a la deriva,
más cerca de Saturno, más lejanos,
mientras el sol da vuelta y nos arrastra
y la sangre recorre su profundo universo
más sagrado que todos los astros.

Estar aquí en la tierra: no más lejos
que un árbol, no más inexplicables;
livianos en otoño, henchidos en verano,
con lo que somos o no somos, con la sombra,
la memoria, el deseo; hasta el fin
(si hay un fin) voz a voz,
casa por casa,
sea quien lleve la tierra, si la llevan,
o quien la espere, si la aguardan,
partiendo juntos cada vez el pan
en dos, en tres, en cuatro
sin olvidar las sombras de la hormiga
que siempre viaja de remotas estrellas
para estar a la hora en nuestra cena
aunque las migas sean amargas.

Terredad

To be here these years on earth
with clouds moving in, birds
suspended in the delicate hours.
On board and all but adrift,
nearer to Saturn and then farther off,
while the sun spins and drags us along
and the blood runs its infinitesimal cosmos,
holier even than the stars.

To be here on earth: no farther off
than a tree, no less explicable;
unburdened in autumn, swollen in summer
with what we are or are not, with darkness,
memory, desire, here till the end
(if end there is) voice to voice,
house by house,
with whoever keeps up the earth, if it's kept up,
or whoever waits, if it's awaited,
dividing the bread together each time
in half, thirds, quarters,
not forgetting the shadows of ants
who journey in always from distant stars
to be here for dinner,
no matter how bitter our crumbs.

La terredad de un pájaro

La terredad de un pájaro es su canto,
lo que en su pecho vuelve al mundo
con los ecos de un coro invisible
desde un bosque ya muerto.
Su terredad es el sueño de encontrarse
en los ausentes,
de repetir hasta el final la melodía
mientras crucen abiertas los aires
sus alas pasajeras;
aunque no sepa a quién le canta
ni por qué,
ni si podrá escucharse en otros algún día
como cada minuto quiso ser:
—más inocente.
Desde que nace nada ya lo aparta
de su deber terrestre;
trabaja al sol, procrea, busca sus migas
y es sólo su voz lo que defiende,
porque en el tiempo no es un pájaro
sino un rayo en la noche de su especie,
una persecución sin tregua de la vida
para que el canto permanezca.

A Bird's *Terredad*

A bird's *terredad* is its song, which
it returns to the world through its breast,
echoing an invisible chorus
from a forest long dead.
Its *terredad* is its dreaming of seeing itself
in those missing,
repeating the tune till the end,
dividing the sky,
its fleeting wings spreading;
and yet it doesn't know who it sings to
or why,
or if it might hear itself someday in others
as it's wanted every minute to be:
more pure.
Since birth nothing has kept it
from its terrestrial duty;
it works by daylight, breeds, seeks its crumbs,
its voice its only defense;
it's not a bird in the end
but a flash in the night of its species,
unceasingly pursuing living
so that the singing remains.

La casa

En la mujer, en lo profundo de su cuerpo
    se construye la casa,
     entre murmullos y silencios.
Hay que acarrear sombras de piedras,
    leves andamios,
     imitar a las aves.

Especialmente cuando duerme
    y en el sueño sonríe
     —nivelar hacia el fondo,
     no despertarla;
seguir el declive de sus formas,
los movimientos de sus manos.

Sobre las dunas que cubren su sueño
    en convulso paisaje,
     hay que elevar altas paredes,
fundar contra la lluvia, contra el viento,
    años y años.

Un ademán a veces fija un muro,
de algún susurro nace una ventana,
desmontamos errantes a la puerta
    y atamos el caballo.

Al fondo de su cuerpo la casa nos espera
y la mesa servida con las palabras limpias
para vivir, tal vez para morir,
    ya no sabemos,
porque al entrar nunca se sale.

House

In the depths of a woman's body
    a house is constructed
    amidst murmurs and pauses.
There are shadows of stones to collect,
    fragile scaffolds,
    imitating the bird.

Above all when she sleeps,
    smiling in dreaming—
    to survey her completely
    don't wake her up;
trace the slope of her hips,
the sweep of her hands.

On the dunes containing her dream,
    turbulent country,
    high walls must be raised
to keep out the rain, and the wind,
    year after year.

A gesture sometimes informs a wall,
from a whisper a window is born,
like nomads we dismount at the door
    and tie up the horse.

In depths of her body the house awaits,
the table fitted with plain words
for living, or dying perhaps,
    no one can say—

nobody who ever enters leaves.

Creo en la vida

Creo en la vida bajo forma terrestre,
tangible, vagamente redonda,
menos esférica en sus polos,
por todas partes llena de horizontes.

Creo en las nubes, en sus páginas
nítidamente escritas
y en los árboles, sobre todo al otoño.
(A veces creo que soy un árbol.)

Creo en la vida como terredad,
como gracia o desgracia.
—Mi mayor deseo fue nacer,
a cada vez aumenta.

Creo en la duda agónica de Dios,
es decir, creo que no creo,
aunque de noche, solo,
interrogo a las piedras,
pero no soy ateo de nada
salvo de la muerte.

I Believe

I believe in life in terrestrial form,
tangible, aimlessly circular,
less round at the ends,
everywhere full of horizons.

I believe in clouds, in their sharply
written sheets
and in trees, above all in autumn.
(At times I believe I'm a tree.)

I believe in life as *terredad*,
as grace or disgrace.
—My highest wish was to be born,
each time expanding.

I believe in the desperate doubt of God,
that is, I believe I do not believe,
although at night, alone,
I question the stones,
and yet I am atheist in nothing
but dying.

Setiembre

a Alejandro Oliveros

Mira setiembre: nada se ha perdido
con fiarnos de las hojas.
La juventud vino y se fue, los árboles no se movieron.
El hermano al morir te quemó en llanto
pero el sol continúa.
La casa fue derrumbada, no su recuerdo.
Mira setiembre con su pala al hombro
cómo arrastra hojas secas.

La vida vale más que la vida, sólo eso cuenta.
Nadie nos preguntó para nacer,
¿qué sabían nuestros padres? ¿Los suyos qué supieron?
Ningún dolor les ahorró sombra y sin embargo
se mezclaron al tiempo terrestre.
Los árboles saben menos que nosotros
y aún no se vuelven.
La tierra va más sola ahora sin dioses
pero nunca blasfema.
Mira setiembre cómo te abre el bosque
y sobrepasa tu deseo.
Abre tus manos, llénalas con estas lentas hojas,
no dejes que una sola se te pierda.

September

for Alejandro Oliveros

Look at September: it has lost nothing
by entrusting its leaves to us.
Youth came and went, the trees didn't budge.
Your brother's dying burned you with weeping
but the sun continues.
The house was destroyed but the memory was not.
Look how September with its blade at its shoulder
drags its dry leaves.

Life is worth more than life, only this matters.
Nobody asked us to be born.
What did our parents know? What did theirs know?
Not a single pain saved them from shadow, and yet
they mingled in their terrestrial hours.
Trees know less than us
and still don't return.
The earth is lonelier now without gods
but refuses to curse.
Look how September opens the forest
and supersedes your desire.
Open your hands, fill them with these slow leaves,
don't let even one pass unnoticed.

El Dorado

a Luis García Morales

Siempre buscábamos El Dorado
en aviones y barcos de vela,
como alquimistas, como Diógenes,
al fin del arco iris,
por los parajes más ausentes.
Unos caían, otros llegaban,
jamás nos detuvimos.
Los hombres del país Orinoco
nunca elegimos otra muerte.

Perdimos años, fuerza, vida;
nadie soñó que iba en la sangre,
que éramos su espejo.
El oro del alma profunda
a través de las voces
que nos inventaban los ríos
en el rumor de las aldeas.
El Dorado que trae el café
a la luz del Caribe
con sus soles a paso de bueyes.
Jamás lo descubrimos,
no era para nosotros su secreto.
Los hombres del país Orinoco
teníamos raza de la quimera.

El Dorado

for Luis García Morales

We sought El Dorado by plane
and sailboat always,
like alchemists, like Diogenes,
at the base of the rainbow,
the most vacant places.
Some of us fell, others went on,
we did not relent.
Men from Orinoco
wouldn't choose other deaths.

We wasted years, energy, vigor;
nobody knew it moved in the blood,
that we had been its reflection.
That the rivers the voices invented
in the murmuring villages
held gold of the deep soul;
that El Dorado brought coffee
slowly, lumbering in Caribbean light
with its gold coins.
We never found it,
its secret wasn't for us.
Men from Orinoco
descend from men of mirage.

Cuando mi estatua se despierte

Cuando mi estatua se despierte
continuará, no obstante, un largo rato
inmóvil, fija,
hasta que cese el coro de los pájaros
que la rodeen cantando en ese instante.
Quieta, sin parpadear, sin que se note
que mi sangre reinicia su curso
por sus venas de mármol,
ha de fingir que está soñando todavía,
que nada siente del vértigo de cosas
donde fluye el paisaje.
No hablará, no dará ni el más leve respiro
mientras sigan en torno los cantos
y tal vez cuando callen se habrá vuelto a dormir,
sin darse cuenta,
debajo del musgo solitario.

When My Statue Awakens

When my statue awakens
it will remain a good while
immobile, still
until the chanting bird choir
surrounding it ceases.
Serene, unblinking, not feeling
my blood beginning to run again
in its marble veins,
it will have to pretend to keep dreaming,
to not to feel the whirl of the world
where the countryside flows.
It won't speak, nor offer the slightest sigh
while the chants around it continue;
perhaps when they stop it will sleep again,
uncomprehending,
under the desolate moss.

Debo estar lejos

Debo estar lejos
porque no oigo los pájaros.
Me ha extraviado la tarde en su vacío,
he recorrido esta ciudad
de voces extranjeras
sólo para advertir cuánto dependo
de sus cantos,
y cómo sus silbos gota a gota
se mezclan en mi sangre.
Debo estar lejos
o los pájaros habrán enmudecido
tal vez adrede,
para que su silencio me regrese
y mis pasos remonten las piedras
en esta larga calle,
hasta que vuelva a oírlos en el viento
y el migratorio corazón se me adormezca
debajo de sus alas.

I Must Be Far Off

I must be far off
because I do not hear the birds.
In the vacuum the afternoon has misled me,
I have sifted this city
of alien tongues
only to notice how much I depend
on their songs,
how the trilling mingles
drop by drop with my blood.
I must be far off
or maybe the birds have gone quiet
on purpose
so that respite might bring me
stepping back over the stones
of this unending street
to hear them again on the wind,
the migrating heart lulling me
in their wings.

From *Trópico absoluto* (1982)

Si vuelvo alguna vez

Si vuelvo alguna vez
será por el canto de los pájaros.
No por los árboles que han de partir conmigo
o irán después a visitarme en el otoño,
ni por los ríos que, bajo tierra,
siguen hablándonos con sus voces más nítidas.
Si al fin regreso corpóreo o incorpóreo,
levitando en mí mismo,
aunque ya nada logre oír desde la ausencia,
sé que mi voz se hallará al lado de sus coros
y volveré, si he de volver, por ellos;
lo que fue vida en mí no cesará de celebrarse,
habitaré el más inocente de sus cantos.

From *Absolute Tropics* (1982)

If I Return Again

If I return again, it will be
for the singing of birds.
Not for the trees that will have to leave
with me, or will visit me later, in autumn,
nor for the underground rivers
addressing us still in their clearest voices.
If I return finally, corporeal or incorporeal,
levitating within,
I may not hear a thing in the vacuum
but my voice will rise with their choirs nonetheless
and I will return, if I have to, for them;
that which was life in me will not fail to celebrate;
I will inhabit their most innocent songs.

Canción

Cada cuerpo con su deseo
y el mar al frente.
Cada lecho con su naufragio
y los barcos al horizonte.

Estoy cantando la vieja canción
que no tiene palabras.
Cada cuerpo junto a otro cuerpo,
cada espejo temblando en la sombra
y las nubes errantes.

Estoy tocando la antigua guitarra
con que los amantes se duermen.
Cada ventana en sus helechos,
cada cuerpo desnudo en su noche
y el mar al fondo, inalcanzable.

Song

Each body with its desire
and the sea just ahead.
Each bed with its shipwreck
and ships on the horizon.

I am singing
the ancient wordless song.
Each body nudging another,
each mirror shaking in shadow,
in wandering clouds.

I play the old guitar
to which the lovers drowse.
Each window with its ferns,
each body naked in its night,
the unreachable sea far below.

Mi país en un mapa antiguo

Nunca mintieron las líneas del cartógrafo
al copiarnos su sueño.
Es cierto que muchos cauces de estos ríos
eran imaginarios,
nuestras montañas no llegan hasta el sur
ni el mar les roza, aunque lo intente,
sus contornos sentimentales.
Es otro el tamaño de las islas
bajo el tacto de sus colores.
Pero fue exacta siempre la piedad
y el fulgor de los ojos asombrados
ante la luz de las palmeras.
¿Qué importa el Orinoco más al norte
prolongado como un deseo,
o esa península con rostro de mujer
que casi habla?
Nunca mintieron: aquí estuvo Manoa
al fin del arco iris que nace en El Dorado
y más allá la infinita inocencia
de un paraíso
que valió todos los viajes de sus naves.
¿Qué otra verdad podemos reclamarles?
Esos mapas eran bellas cartas de amor,
tatuajes de navegantes,
páginas puras para decirnos que la vida
sólo es eterna en esta orilla del Atlántico.

My Country on an Ancient Map

The cartographer's lines never lied,
tracing his dream for us.
Many of these river channels
were fabled, for sure:
our mountains don't stretch so far south
nor does the sea brush their hopeful foothills,
though it would like to.
The size of the islands is something else
in the swell of his colors.
But the devotion and glow
of astonished eyes was always precise
in the brilliance of palms.
So what if the Orinoco flows
like desire farther north,
or if this cape is misplaced, with its face
of a woman seeming ready to speak?
They never lied: here stood Manoa
at the end of the rainbow that rose from El Dorado,
and farther off, the infinite innocence
of a paradise
that made all its vessels' journeys worthwhile.
What other truth might we extract?
The maps were graceful love letters,
sailors' tattoos,
unstained pages telling us life
is eternal only at this edge of the Atlantic.

Hombres sin nieve

a Carlos Tortolero

Somos los hombres sin nieve
nacidos entre tormentas caniculares,
con las casas abiertas de par en par
y las retinas contraídas
frente al motín incesante de los colores.

Nuestra vida está escrita
por la mano del sol
en las mágicas hojas de la malanga.
Sobre estas tierras no ha nevado en muchos siglos,
esquiamos en la luna, desde lejos,
con largavistas,
sin helarnos la sangre.

Aquí el invierno nace de heladas subjetivas
lleno de ráfagas salvajes;
depende de una mujer que amamos y se aleja,
de sus cartas que no vendrán pero se aguardan;
nos azota de pronto en largas avenidas
cuando nos queman sus hielos impalpables.
Aquí el invierno puede llegar a cualquier hora,
no exige leños, frazadas, abrigos,
no despoja los árboles,
y sin embargo cómo sabe caer bajo cero,
cómo nos hacen tiritar sus témpanos amargos.

Men Without Snow

for Carlos Tortolero

We are men without snow,
born in tempestuous heat,
our houses wide open,
eyes contracted
against an uninterrupted riot of color.

Our lives are written
by the sun's hand
on the spellbound blades of grass.
It hasn't snowed here in centuries—
we ski on the moon, at a remove,
using binoculars,
so our blood doesn't freeze.

Here winter comes in subjective frosts,
rife with savage gusts;
it depends on a woman we love who left,
on her letters we wait for that do not appear;
it stings us suddenly on long boulevards,
burns us with impalpable ice.
Here winter can arrive at any hour,
no firewood, jackets, blankets are needed,
it doesn't strip leaves from trees,
and yet the farther it falls below zero
the more its bitter ice makes us shake.

La durmiente

La que amo duerme lejos, en otro país,
en otro mundo,
aunque su cuerpo al lado me acompaña.
Cierra los ojos y desaparece,
se va, la noche me la niega,
no hay aviones que lleguen adonde se dirige,
ninguna palabra me borra su silencio.
La que amo ya no se ve en el horizonte,
palpo sus manos, sus pies y no la alcanzo,
cruza la sombra y se me pierde . . .
Su cuerpo está conmigo pero adentro no hay nadie,
es una casa sola,
una casa olvidada, desierta,
y no obstante en el fondo, si me asomo,
una llama dorada titila
y nunca se apaga.

She Who Sleeps

She who I love sleeps far away, in another country,
another world,
though her body beside me accompanies me.
She shuts her eyes and disappears,
leaves, night takes her away from me,
planes don't fly where she is heading,
no word undoes her stillness.
She who I love isn't on the horizon,
I touch her hands, feet, but can't reach her,
she crosses the dark, lost to me . . .
Her body is with me but no one's inside,
she's an empty house,
a house forgotten, abandoned,
and yet if I lean close to look
a gold flame flutters
that will not be extinguished.

No es de nosotros el amor

No es de nosotros el amor, es de los cuerpos
que se desnudan en su música táctil
y aquí nos dejan abandonados.
Al reunirse en el relámpago de Dios,
ya no aceptan acompañantes.
Somos como los trajes que se quitan,
como las sombras caídas de su lámpara.
Después se alejan nimbados del deseo
que hace girar la tierra,
mientras con sorda envidia contemplamos
ojos y labios que se mezclan,
voces y besos que vuélvense susurros.
Nada queda de ti, de mí, cuando se juntan;
somos los ríos donde rodaron como leños,
los secos cauces que se borran, las agujas
de algún reloj atormentado dando vueltas
frente a su instante eterno.

From *Alphabet of the World* (1986)

Love Isn't Ours

Love isn't ours but belongs to our bodies,
which undress in love's tactile music
and abandon us here.
When they meet in God's lightning
they allow no companions.
We're like suits they remove,
like shadows flung from their lamp.
Later they leave, haloed with the desire
that keeps the earth turning,
while with deaf envy we contemplate
eyes and lips mingling,
voices and kisses dropping to whispers.
Nothing remains of you, of me, when they meet;
we're the rivers where they rolled like logs,
the dry ditches that vanish, the hands
of some tormented clock circling,
facing their undying instant.

Vidamagia

Tráenos el mar de ayer que nunca miente,
sin derramar ni una gota de sus olas.
Doblado cabe en esta alcoba el horizonte
junto a las nubes que siempre lo despliegan.
Basta un velero al fondo, un solo grito
de la gaviota más salvaje.
Tira las islas por la ventana.

Trae a la niña rubia que en la arena
jugaba con nosotros. No importa que su cuerpo
nada retenga del júbilo inocente.
Que venga con su tedio, su adulterio,
y el recado del último analista.
Algo podrá salvar si se zambulle
desnuda entre las aguas.

Y no olvides el tren contento de echar humo
que llevó a Juan una mañana al puerto
en la época de Lindbergh.
—¡Trae el avión de Lindbergh!
Ante el azul no existe el tiempo ni la muerte
y en nuestro espejo cabe siempre otro mar
mucho más grande, oleando a su deseo.
Que todo vuelva entre las rocas y palmeras
de nuestro viejo mar que nunca miente.
Tira tu sombra por la ventana.

Magic Life

Bring us the sea we knew that never deceives
and don't spill a drop as it breaks.
The horizon fits folded up in this room
with the clouds that crease it forever.
A sailboat in the distance is plenty, the lone cry
of the wildest gull.
Throw islands out the window.

Bring on the blonde little girl in the sand
who played with us once. Who cares if her body
holds nothing now of that innocent joy?
Let her boredom arise, her adultery,
the words of her most recent therapist.
Something here can be saved if she slips
naked into the waves.

And don't forget the train happily spewing smoke
that carried Juan to the harbor one morning
during the Lindbergh days.
—Bring on Lindbergh's plane!
In view of the blue, death and time don't exist
and our mirror holds always another
much bigger ocean, breaking at whim.
May it all return among the rocks and palms
of our ancient sea which never deceives.
Throw your shadow out the window.

Trastiempo

¿Quién me cambió los pasos que me llevan
por esta calle de rostros desconocidos?
Ya las casas no son las mismas;
se oye un eco distinto en las palabras;
este lunes quizá sea martes;
el mar, sobre todo, parece aquí muy lejos.
Sin percatarme, en tanto tiempo,
a la orilla de un río que ya no existe
me he quedado dormido.

¿En qué mes de qué siglo erraba absorto
escuchando unos pájaros ya ausentes?
Esa ventana no estaba allí;
en el espejo miro unos ojos que no son míos.
¿Cuándo escribí aquel falso poema
que lleva mi firma?
Desesperado busco a tientas por el mundo
mis huellas sonámbulas.
¿A dónde huyó mi juventud? —Ya no lo sé.
Me ha dejado aquí solo y se fue por el río.

Beyond Time

How did my feet find their way
to this street of strange faces?
The houses now are not as they were;
one hears other echoes in words;
Monday is Tuesday, perhaps;
the sea, above all, seems a long way from here.
I hadn't guessed I'd been asleep
for so long on the edge of a river
that no longer exists.

In which month in which century did I wander
distracted, hearing those now absent birds?
This window here wasn't there;
in the mirror the eyes I see aren't mine.
When did I write that false poem
bearing my name?
In despair I feel my way through the world
seeking my somnambulant footprints.
Where did my youth go? —I don't know now.
It's left me alone here and gone down the river.

En esta calle

En esta calle soy más joven que en las otras;
aquí a mi paso las ramas de caobos
desentierran un cobrizo color de horas estáticas,
dejando que mi edad mude sus sombras
y entre las voces de quienes van o vuelven
me reconozca menos solitario.

Hoy por ejemplo, al ir bajo la lluvia,
algo de mí que sólo queda en los retratos
volvió a rodearme de repente
como una sombra que me llevaba lejos.
Sentí en mi voz de nuevo un eco antiguo
y hablando, calle abajo, entre las piedras,
crucé despacio los troncos renegridos,
la rumorosa hilera de caobos.
No sé quién iba escuchándome en la lluvia
ni qué decía . . .
                    Pero no hablaba solo.

On This Street

On this street I'm younger than on others;
the mahogany limbs I pass as I walk
restore the copper tints of static hours,
letting years shed the shadows
and amidst voices of those going
and coming I find I'm less lonely.

Today in fact heading out in the rain,
something in me remaining only in pictures
besieged me again suddenly
like a shadow that pulled me away.
I felt an old echo in my voice again
and calling out down the block, crossed by
the stones slowly, past the blackened trunks,
the murmuring rows of mahoganies.
I don't know who was listening in the rain
or what I said . . .
                    But I wasn't speaking alone.

Mi lámpara

De noche, al apagarla, en mi silencio
puedo oírla rezar.
Cansada ya de arder, de tanto estar en vela
frente a la oscuridad del mundo,
ruega no sé en qué lengua solitaria
por ti, por mí, por todos los que doblan
atormentados el último periódico
y en sueño apartan la sombra de sus letras,
como quien ya no indaga, aunque le importe,
cuánta vida nos guarda la tierra todavía
cuando mañana se despierte.

My Lantern

At night, putting it out, I hear it pray
in my silence.
Tired now of burning, keeping vigil
so long in the dark of the world,
it prays in I don't know which lonely language—
for you, for me, for all those who crease
the latest newspaper, tormented,
and dreaming, divide shadow from print,
they who no longer consider, although it matters,
how much life the earth holds for us still
after tomorrow appears.

Letras

Un día este rostro era la vida
pero se inclinó tanto entre los libros
que poco a poco, sin notarlo,
mudó mi carne en letras.
Hoy el espejo en sus azogues lo dibuja
—un libro más, perdido, mal impreso:
E la nariz, Z la oreja, T los párpados;
en el mentón dos o tres sílabas sin barba;
la frente en W cortada a medias
por un gorro de fieltro hecho una Q.
Entre los ojos miopes alternan una S, y una R
　　　　　(¡con diéresis!)
y siete o más vocales indescifrables.
Sólo la boca queda en blanco
y su repliegue finge un garabato
con la dureza de esos gritos
que no se dejan traducir a tinta o sangre.

Letters

This face was everything once
but it bent so much into books
that little by little, imperceptibly,
its flesh turned to letters.
Today the mirror depicts it in fits—
another derelict book, poorly printed:
an E for the nose, Z for an ear, T for eyelids;
two or three syllables, whiskerless, comprise
the chin; the W forehead, bisected
by a felt cap that forms a Q.
Between these nearsighted eyes an S and R alternate
            (in dieresis!)
joined by seven or more indecipherable vowels.
Only the mouth remains blank
though its crease seems a sign
of those petrified cries
one can't translate in ink or blood.

Escritura

Alguna vez escribiré con piedras,
midiendo cada una de mis frases
por su peso, volumen, movimiento.
Estoy cansado de palabras.

No más lápiz: andamios, teodolitos,
la desnudez solar del sentimiento
tatuando en lo profundo de las rocas
su música secreta.

Dibujaré con líneas de guijarros
mi nombre, la historia de mi casa
y la memoria de aquel río
que va pasando siempre y se demora
entre mis venas como sabio arquitecto.

Con piedra viva escribiré mi canto
en arcos, puentes, dólmenes, columnas,
frente a la soledad del horizonte,
como un mapa que se abra ante los ojos
de los viajeros que no regresan nunca.

Writing

Someday I'll write with stones,
measuring each of my phrases
by weight, volume, motion.
I've had it with words.

No pencils: scaffolding, surveying,
the elemental bareness of feeling
imprinting its deep secret music
in the hearts of rocks.

I'll draw my name with rows
of pebbles, draw the history of my home
and the memory of that river
which passes by always and hangs
in my veins like a wise engineer.

With living stone I'll write my song—
in arches, bridges, stone tombs, columns—
facing the horizon's solitude
like a map opening itself to the eyes
of travelers who never return.

Alfabeto del mundo

En vano me demoro deletreando
el alfabeto del mundo.
Leo en las piedras un oscuro sollozo,
ecos ahogados en torres y edificios,
indago la tierra por el tacto
llena de ríos, paisajes y colores,
pero al copiarlos siempre me equivoco.
Necesito escribir ciñéndome a una raya
sobre el libro del horizonte.
Dibujar el milagro de esos días
que flotan envueltos en la luz
y se desprenden en cantos de pájaros.
Cuando en la calle los hombres que deambulan
de su rencor a su fatiga, cavilando,
se me revelan más que nunca inocentes.
Cuando el tahúr, el pícaro, la adúltera,
los mártires del oro o del amor
son sólo signos que no he leído bien,
que aún no logro anotar en mi cuaderno.
Cuánto quisiera al menos un instante
que esta plana febril de poesía
grabe en su transparencia cada letra:
la o del ladrón, la t del santo
el gótico diptongo del cuerpo y su deseo,
con la misma escritura del mar en las arenas,
la misma cósmica piedad
que la vida despliega ante mis ojos.

Alphabet of the World

In vain I consider spelling out
the alphabet of the world.
I read in rocks an obscure sobbing,
choked echoes in towers and buildings;
I sift earth full of rivers, scenery, shades,
but always in transcribing, fail.
I need to adhere as I write to a line
on the book of the horizon.
To sketch the miracle of these days
that float sealed in light
and surrender in birdsong.
The men in the street who wander
from bitter to weary, brooding,
appear to me more innocent than ever.
The gambler, the picaro, adulteress,
the martyrs of gold or love
are merely signs that I have read poorly,
that I have yet to fill out in my notebook.
How much I've wanted just an instant
to let this feverish sheet of verse
record each letter in its transparency:
the *e* of the thief, the *t* of the saint,
the muted plosive of *body* with all its desire,
in the same hand as that of the sea on the sand,
with the same cosmic pity
that life lays bare for my eyes.

Honor al asno

Honor al asno por la estrella
que su ignorancia nos alumbra.
Por la lenta soledad pétrea,
tan dócil y tan útil.
Honor al asno que lleva al poeta
a lo largo del mundo,
aguzando sus largas orejas
ante todos los versos,
cualquiera sea la música.
Honor al asno, a su baúl de mariposas,
donde guarda los golpes de Dios y de los hombres
y no se queja nunca.

Honor the Ass

Honor the ass for the star
of stupidity by which he illuminates.
For his slow petrified solitude,
so docile and useful.
Honor the ass that carries the poet
along through the world,
pricking his long ears
before each of his lines,
whatever the music.
Honor the ass, honor his box of butterflies,
where he stores the blows of God and men
and never complains.

El molino

Gira tus aspas, viejo molino,
muele sin tregua las horas de estos días,
aventando su cáscara.
Borra las letras del poema en que he mentido,
la palabra que no nació como una uña
de mi carne
y la guitarra negra de mi sombra
que nunca canta cuando viaja.
Muele este cuarto lleno de libros,
pulveriza sus muros piedra por piedra
hasta que la ventana se eleve como un pájaro
y en sus alas volando me lleve.
No te quedes inmóvil a la orilla del mundo
entre mis ojos y el paisaje.

The Mill

Turn your blades, old mill,
grind without pause the hours of these days,
tossing off husks.
Erase the poems in which I lied,
words that didn't rise like fingernails
from my flesh
and the black guitar of my shadow,
failing to sing as it goes.
Grind this room full of books,
crush its walls stone by stone
until the window lifts like a bird
and bears me off on its wings.
Continue to turn at the edge of the world
between my eyes and the wild field.

La hora de Hamlet

Esta mañana me sorprende
con mi olvidada calavera entre las manos.
Hago de Hamlet.

Es la hora reductiva del monólogo
en que interrogo a mi Hacedor
sobre esta máscara que ha de volverse polvo,
sobre este polvo que sigue hablando todavía
aquí y acaso en otra parte.

A la distancia que me encuentre de la muerte,
hago de Hamlet.

Hamlet y pájaro con vértigo de alturas,
tras las almenas del íngrimo castillo
que cada quien erige piedra a piedra
para ser o no ser según la suerte,
el destino, la sombra, los pasos del fantasma.

Hamlet's Hour

Morning surprised me
with the forgotten skull in my hands.
I'm playing Hamlet.

It's the essential hour of the speech
in which I question my Maker
about this mask that must rejoin the dust,
about the dust that keeps speaking after—
here and perhaps elsewhere.

From whichever distance death may approach,
I'm playing Hamlet.

Hamlet and a bird sickened by heights
over the ramparts of the lonely castle
each of us builds, rock by rock,
to be or not to be according to luck,
fate, darkness, the steps of the ghost.

La poesía

La poesía cruza la tierra sola,
apoya su voz en el dolor del mundo
y nada pide
                    —ni siquiera palabras.

Llega de lejos y sin hora, nunca avisa;
tiene la llave de la puerta.
Al entrar siempre se detiene a mirarnos.
Después abre su mano y nos entrega
una flor o un guijarro, algo secreto,
pero tan intenso que el corazón palpita
demasiado veloz. Y despertamos.

Poetry

Poetry traverses the earth alone,
investing its voice in the pain of the world;
it asks for nothing—
                            not even words.

It arrives from far off at whatever hour
without warning; it's got the key to the door.
Coming in, it will pause always to study us.
Later it opens its hand and delivers
a flower, or pebble, something secret
but so intense the heart beats
too quickly. And we awaken.

Av. Duque de Loulé

Y la mañana abrió a Lisboa
en su gran libro de piedras blancas
que mi corazón no había leído.
Flotaban casas en la niebla,
ventanas con el coro de sus voces
y muros altos tallados en el iris.
Quise leerla como los ciegos, por el tacto,
no a la intemperie sino dentro de mí mismo,
errando de lo visible a lo invisible,
donde la mañana la volcaba,
donde su luz iba llenándome las venas
y me arrastraban las velas de sus barcos
y yo era su dominio.

Avenue Duque de Loulé

And morning opened Lisbon
with its great book of white stones
my heart hadn't read.
Houses floated in the mist,
windows with their chorus of voices,
tall walls engraved by rainbows.
I wanted to read as if blind, feelingly,
not from without but within,
wandering from the visible to invisible,
where morning had spilled it,
where its light swelled my veins
and sails of boats drew me on
and I was commanded.

Vísperas de viaje

De nuevo un viaje moviendo de raíz
mi cuerpo como un barco,
de nuevo el grito de otro ignoto horizonte.
Tensos llevo los nervios como jarcias;
las valijas que por años invernaron
puntuales a esta hora se despiertan.
A babor y estribor crece el azoramiento
de pasarelas y silbatos,
aprestos de partida, cosas que se nos quedan.
Difícil escribir a bordo una palabra,
el corazón, sobresaltado, miente.
Mis libros otra vez con sus ojos de perro
me acompañan hasta la puerta.
Quisiera decir adiós con una sola sílaba,
la menos dolorosa,
la más breve.

On the Eve of Embarking

Again like a ship a journey moves
the depths of my body,
again the cry of a foreign horizon.
I hold my nerves taut as ropes;
suitcases that hibernated for years
now awaken on cue.
Confusion swells in gangplanks
and whistles, port and starboard,
the bustle to go, the things we abandon.
It's hard to write one word on board—
the heart, mid-somersault, lies.
Once more my books with their dogs' eyes
follow me to the door.
I wanted to say goodbye in a single syllable,
least painfully,
quickly.

From *Partitura de la cigarra* (1999)

Al retorno

No sé si entonces era otoño,
el apócrifo otoño de estos trópicos,
no guardo rastro de esos días.
De cualquier estación, sea la que fuere,
no queda por caer hoja ninguna.
La vida jugó sus propias cartas:
—nada salió, tal vez, como yo quise
ni dejó de salir como no quise,
porque no quise nada.
Tras tantos años vuelvo a reencontrarme
con lo que queda, si algo queda,
de la ciudad que amaron mis mayores
al pie de esta montaña.
En la hojarasca se oyen murmullos de oro
que amontona la tarde.
Pronto hará frío.
El Ávila me salve.

From *The Cicada's Score* (1999)

Coming Back

It may have been autumn then,
the false autumn of the tropics,
I don't know, those days are lost to me.
Whichever season, whatever occurred,
not a single leaf is left to fall.
Life dealt its own cards:
nothing turned out as I wanted, perhaps,
nor did it not turn out as I wanted
because I wanted nothing at all.
After so many years I'm meeting again
that which remains, if something remains,
of the city my ancestors loved
at the foot of this mountain.
One hears in dead leaves the gold murmurs
the afternoon gathers.
It will be cold soon.
May the Ávila save me.

La puerta

Nada de nieve en esta puerta,
sólo calor, madera que se dilata
y cantos de cigarras.
No nieva dentro ni fuera de la casa,
ni siquiera la pluma del lorito
que cae sin vanidad, es fría o blanca.
Nada de nieve: patios soleados,
rostros perplejos en retratos de paredes,
tensos anturios rojos en macetas.
. . . Y la puerta atascada
de tanta nieve no caída
que siempre sigue no cayendo
hasta que todo este calor se vuelve frío.

Door

No sign of snow at the door,
only heat, swelling wood
and songs of cicadas.
No snow inside or outside the house,
nor is the parrot's feather, drifting
unassumingly down, icy or white.
No sign of snow: sun-drenched patios,
puzzled faces on posters on walls,
taut red tail-flowers in pots.
... And the door obstructed
by so much unfallen snow,
by snow forever failing to fall
until all this heat starts to freeze.

Final de lluvia

Ya ennegrecen los árboles
sus ramas y sus flores
al fin del aguacero.

En la terraza del Café
una sombra amontona las sillas
donde rondan amores bisiestos.

Las últimas gotas en las hojas
lavan las plumas del tordo
que ya por hoy no quiere vuelo.

Pasan parejas con paraguas.
Pasan paraguas sin parejas.

End of Rain

The limbs and blooms
of the trees are dark now
at the end of the downpour.

Under the overhang at the café
dimness gathers the chairs
where haphazard love lingers.

The last runnels on leaves
soak the wings of the starling;
for the moment it opts not to fly.

Couples pass with umbrellas.
Umbrellas pass without couples.

Un sapo

De salto en salto, cortándome el camino,
un viejo sapo se abalanza,
croando sin cesar, ronco y agreste.
Llega de no sé dónde a interponerse
en medio de la noche y se engulle mis horas,
mis horas que son grillos, crisálidas, coleópteros,
mis horas que sin él serían estrellas . . .

Mi doble cruel, mi sórdido enemigo,
cada instante me empuja a su pantano
con su cara de sapo que no es sapo
sino otro bulto de mi sombra,
el lado punitivo de mi carne,
el que arruga la piel y me encanece,
—éste que escribe ahora con mi lápiz
y me reduce el año a mes, el mes a día,
el que tras cada salto me anonada
y con mi propia boca dice a gritos: ¡yo!

Toad

Plodding up, obstructing my path,
an old toad pauses,
ragged and hoarse, unendingly croaking.
He rolls in from nowhere at midnight
to plant himself here to gobble my hours,
these hours that are crickets, winged beetles, grubs,
hours that without him might have been stars . . .

Cruel double, unsightly foe,
moment by moment nudging me into his swamp
with his toad's face that's not so much toad
as another lump in my shadow,
that punishing part of me
creasing my skin, making me gray—
the part that writes now with my pen,
cutting a year to a month, a month to a day,
that which with each hop renders me dumb
but shouts with my mouth: *me!*

Medianoche

Escribo tarde. Es medianoche.
Ignoro cuándo he remontado este camino,
cómo llegué donde me encuentro, qué buscaba.
La Cruz del Sur ya se ha corrido al centro
de la radiante soledad nocturna.
No estoy seguro aquí de nada, ni de estos gallos
que alrededor se desgañitan.
Escribo tarde. Los gallos cantan demasiado,
cantan por Esculapio, por Sócrates, por Cristo
y por el viejo Eduardo,
a quien siempre despiertan en su tumba
para que distribuya ahora sus gritos
como si fueran las migas de un relámpago.

Midnight

I write late. It's midnight.
I don't know when I made it up to this road,
how I landed where I find myself now, what I sought.
The Southern Cross has passed at the heart
of this brilliant nocturnal quiet.
Here I am certain of nothing, not even these roosters
shrieking around me.
I write late. The roosters sing without cease,
they sing for Asclepius, Socrates, Christ,
and old Edward, whom they rouse again
in his tomb; he scatters their cries now
like flecks of leftover lightning.

Escrito de paso

El poeta no canta, cruza la calle.
Vuelan autos y sombras
a la velocidad del pánico.
Viejas estatuas parpadean.
Taxis llenos de momias
se dirigen a las pirámides.
Una luna veloz,
patria de Nefertitis,
huye del minotauro.

El poeta viaja de un verso a otro
entre semáforos vocálicos.
No canta ahora, sería inútil,
esquiva la sombra y el vértigo
sin pronunciar palabra.
Bajo esta larga noche
su voz es un relámpago
que está alumbrando ahora en otra parte.

Written in Passing

The poet doesn't sing, he crosses
the street. Autos and shadows
fly by at panic speed.
Ancient statues twitch.
Taxis jammed with mummies
make their way to the pyramids.
An agile moon,
home to Nefertiti,
is pursued by the minotaur.

The poet travels one line to another
between traffic-light vowels.
He doesn't sing, it would be useless,
he dodges dimness and madness
without uttering a word.
In this long night
his voice is lightning
that is creating heat elsewhere.

From *Papiros amorosos* (2002)

Aquí

Aquí, amor mío, se queda el canto,
aquí se quedan las palabras . . .
Y la dicha veloz de esta esfera volando
detrás de un sol que nos ignora
y nos arrastra hacia su noche,
aquí también sin huella ha de apagarse.

Aquí, amor mío, nos desvestimos;
los cuerpos quedan solos con sus sombras,
las sombras con el viento,
mientras la luna salva lo que puede
de todo el íntimo naufragio.

Mas aunque se adueñe del olvido
el soplo que nos borra,
algo de ti, de mí quizá se salve
y aquí perdure en el azul terrestre.
Aquí, amor mío, con esta lámpara
que propaga el claror de su luz nómada,
aquí donde otras sombras que no vemos
también nos acompañan.

From *Love Parchments* (2002)

Here

Here, my love, the song lingers,
and here linger words . . .
And the passing joy of this flying sphere
drawn behind its oblivious sun
dragging us on into night—
this too must dissolve without trace.

Here, my love, we undress;
our bodies linger alone with their shadows
and their shadows with wind
while the moon saves all it can
of this intimate shipwreck.

Even if the gust that undoes us
is dimmed in oblivion,
something of you, maybe of me will be saved
and survive here on the blue earth.
Here, my love, as this lamp
spreads its lucidity of nomad light,
here where other shadows we don't see
move with us also.

Estrellas

Só a dor e as estrêlas
são universais.

Cassiano Ricardo

En la noche, desnuda, rotan sobre tu carne
repentinas estrellas;
circunvalan el aro de tu ombligo,
visten el verde de tu risa,
la luz de tu alegría.
Estrellas en tus hombros, tu cintura,
estrellas en tu sexo,
titilan llenándote los ojos, los cabellos.
Algunas no han nacido y son visibles,
otras ya se extinguieron, pero alumbran.
Te siguen en la sombra, te acompañan,
son ávidas, errantes, cariciosas,
giran sobre el silencio de tu cuerpo,
hallan en ti su bóveda, su casa,
viajan en la constelación de tu deseo.

Stars

*Só a dor e as estrêlas
são universais.*

Cassiano Ricardo

At night, stars spin suddenly
over your naked body;
they circle the ring of your navel,
adorn your evergreen laugh,
the light of your joy.
Stars on your shoulders, hips,
stars on your groin,
the shining animating your eyes and hair.
Some are not yet born but appear,
others are extinguished already but glow.
They follow your shadow, flow with you,
eager, capricious, caressing,
spinning over your body's silence;
they find their chapel in you, home,
traversing the constellation of your desire.

La nieve

Sentí caer cerca de ti la nieve,
la vi cubrir tu cuerpo hasta la sombra,
te llenó el pelo, los hombros, las pestañas . . .
Una nieve que hablaba en un idioma
por mí desconocido.

¿Desde qué mundo bajaba hasta tus senos,
hasta el cóncavo sello de tu ombligo,
si aquí nunca nevó desde milenios?

¿Era nieve en verdad, talco o harina
—la vieja harina de mi casa—,
cayendo sin caer sobre las cosas
con un susurro opaco?

No sé. No me importó sentirla extraña
ni palpar la blancura de sus copos,
sino avivar un fuego ante tus ojos,
alguna llama que crezca con la noche,
aunque la nieve prosiga hablando sola
sobre tu piel, las cumbres, los caminos
de lo que nadie sabe.

Snow

I felt the snow fall around you,
saw it shroud your body in shadow,
bury your hair, shoulders, eyelashes . . .
A snow that spoke in a language
unknown to me.

From which world did it drift to your breasts,
the concave seal of your navel,
when it hasn't snowed for millennia here?

Was it snow, really, or talc or flour—
familiar flour from home—
falling without falling over everything
with its opaque whisper?

I don't know. Strange it felt, touching
that blankness of flakes, but who cared;
better to stir fire under your eyes,
a flame that might rise in the night
though the snow would go on speaking alone
on your skin, on those ridges and roads
which no one comprehends.

El hacha blanca

Y a quien no siente,
¿de qué le sirven las palabras?
Al sin amor, su cuerpo ¿qué le vale?
La noche cae. ¿A quién la sombra importa
si no encuentra una voz que lo acompañe?
La luna alumbra. ¿Qué sueña ahora solo
quien palpó en una piel todos sus rayos?

La ciudad es recta, de paredes vítreas,
autómatas las sombras de sus calles.
En no sé cuál de tantos edificios,
tras alguna ventana, quedan tus ojos
y la música móvil de tus párpados
y en una balanza tus senos,
cuyo fiel es la luna y su hacha blanca . . .

Estoy sintiendo todo lo que vivo
porque tras estas piedras sigo tu sombra
y me acompañan las palabras.
Atravieso la noche y siento las estrellas,
siento demasiado las estrellas
y tus manos, tu boca, tu perfume . . .
Jamás un cuerpo me unió tanto a los astros.

White Axe

What good are words
to a person who doesn't feel?
What good a body to someone unloved?
Night falls. To whom does the dark matter
without a voice there to share it?
The moon brightens. Who dreams alone now,
having felt all its beams in one skin?

The city is linear, walled in glass,
its shadows automatons on the streets.
In one of these buildings,
behind a particular window, your eyes remain,
and the migrant music of your eyelids,
and in balance, your breasts,
their crux the moon and its white axe . . .

I'm feeling all I am living
because over these stones I follow your shadow
and words keep me company.
I cross the night and feel the stars,
feeling too much, too many stars,
and your hands, your lips, your perfume . . .
Never has a body tied me so to the sky.

Otro milenio

Hilo mis frases de amor
a la intemperie,
bajo los árboles de muda historia.

Juan Sánchez Peláez

El milenio que llega divide en dos la noche:
a un lado y otro quedan nuestros cuerpos
y todo lo que amamos uno en otro . . .
Queda la amarga luna errando a ciegas,
Ella y su sombra en nuestros ojos,
ella y lo que no sabemos de este mundo.
Y el amor con su lámpara
que inquiere titilando cuántas horas
nos guardan los relojes todavía.
Y queda, en fin, la tornadiza tierra
que ignora meridianos y milenios
y sigue siempre rotando, tenazmente,
para que nuestros cuerpos de nuevo se reúnan
y noche a noche a bordo se acompañen
en el éter intacto.

Another Millennium

I thread my lines of love
in open air,
under the trees of mute history.

Juan Sánchez Peláez

The arriving millennium divides the night in two:
our bodies remain, one on one side and one on the other,
and all we love each in the other . . .
The bitter moon remains, wandering blind,
the moon and its shade in our eyes,
that and what we can't understand of this world.
And love, too, with its light
wondering in quivers how many hours
our clocks hold yet for us.
And finally the fickle earth remains,
not conscious of meridians and millenniums,
tenacious, rotating forever,
so our bodies might unite again
and floating night after night meet
in the untouched ether.

From *Fábula del escriba* (2006)

Lejos, allá en el siglo XX

Lejos, allá en el siglo XX, entre sus crueles días,
cuando Holan, el checo, afilaba la espuela de su gallo
para que hubiera un canto,
un canto audible aun en las estrellas,
un largo grito seco, subitáneo,
contra las sombras de la noche
y por su patria.

Lejos, cerca de Praga, en medio de la nieve,
cuando su ronco gallo cantaba en griego
sus acordes de quinta,
Holan, insomne, al lado de su lámpara
se encomendaba a Hamlet
y con su príncipe y su gallo,
junto a la llama de aquel grito
y la chispa de sus espuelas,
iba encendiendo cigarro tras cigarro . . .

From *The Scribe's Fable* (2006)

Way Off in the Twentieth Century

Way off in the twentieth century, in the cruel days
when Holan the Czech sharpened his rooster's spur
so he'd have a song,
a song even the stars heard,
a long dry shriek breaking
the shadows of night
for the sake of his country.

Way off near Prague, covered in snow,
then when his cock rasped
its chord fifths in Greek,
Holan, sleepless beside his lamp
entrusted himself to Hamlet,
and with his prince and cock
and the flame from the shriek
and spark from its spurs,
lit cigarette after cigarette . . .

En el paraíso

Cuando fui serpiente,
cuando era liviano mi verde veneno,
a hurtadillas, reptando, llegué al paraíso.
Y al macho empujé hacia la hembra,
hasta unir sus cuerpos, sus nombres, sus noches
en un solo bulto de música táctil.

Con lumbre irisada del viejo deseo
—luz de pavos reales—
fui atando en silencio sus cuerpos,
piernas en las piernas, labios en los labios,
brazos en los brazos . . .
Y yo su serpiente, su nudo, su abismo,
entre hierbas suaves y paradisiales.

Tendidos, sedientos, un cuerpo en el otro
y ambos enlazados,
sin sentir en torno mi sombra huidiza,
mi veneno bífido que los envolvía y los extasiaba,
mezclando su sangre, sus bocas, sus vidas
en un solo cielo de noche en la tierra,
con estos anillos que me dio Saturno
los enamoraba y los envolvía en la maravilla
de tanto milagro.

In Paradise

When I was a serpent,
when my green venom was ripe,
sneaking and snaking I landed in Paradise.
And I shoved the stud toward the bitch,
uniting their bodies, names, nights
in a single shape of palpable music.

With the iridescent fire of ancient desire
—light of peacocks—
I tethered their bodies in silence,
leg to leg, lip to lip,
arm to arm . . .
and I their serpent, their knot, their abyss,
among soft paradisial grasses.

Strung out, parched, one body in another
and both bound,
neither feeling my fleeing shadow about them
or forked tongue that held and entranced,
mixing blood, mouths, lives
in a single heaven of night on earth,
with those rings Saturn gave me
I seduced and held them in wonder
of plentiful miracle.

Hablo y deshablo

Hablo y deshablo en este país caluroso
de mucho mar y pocos barcos.
El horizonte es recto allá a lo lejos
y curvo al navegarlo.
He escuchado por décadas enteras
su inmenso azul en una sola sílaba,
pero siempre repite lo mismo
y no cambia.

Hablo y deshablo entre paisajes que deambulan
detrás de senderos inalcanzables.
Los árboles veloces se cimbran en el viento
y parten a caballo.
Lo demás es el vaho soleado en las marismas
donde la rosa tiene forma de sapo
y es un cúmulo de pétalos que croan
con su cáliz carnívoro al acecho,
la lengua retráctil del pistilo
y el perfume letal de los pantanos.

I Speak and Unspeak

I speak and unspeak in this hot land
that's all sea and few ships.
The horizon is straight in the distance
and curved upon navigating.
I have heard for whole decades
its immense blue in a single syllable,
but it repeats the same thing forever,
unchanging.

I speak and unspeak in wandering settings
on unending paths.
Speeding trees shake in the wind
and tear off on horseback.
The rest is sunlit mist in the wetlands
where the rose is shaped like a toad
and it's a cluster of petals that croaks
with its carnivorous calyx cocked,
the retractile tongue of the pistil
and lethal perfume of swamps.

Gramática de la ausencia

a Miguel Gomes

Ya no quiero volver a aquella calle
donde las casas demolidas
siguen en pie.

Ni tampoco leer en esta hora
esos poemas míos
que estoy seguro de no haber escrito.

Y al fin, ¿de qué me sirve
volver de nuevo a la rue de Turenne,
si aquellos barcos en que viajaba
nunca partieron?

La gramática de la ausencia
declina voces tan amargas
que siempre significan otra cosa
sin que nos demos cuenta.

Por eso mi trato con el mundo
prefiere el pospretérito,
sin creerse raíz
ni desinencia.

Y acaso lo mejor sea ver la lluvia
cayendo sin cesar sobre los techos,
aunque la calle al sol siga más seca.
Entonces llueve pero no llueve,
es decir, ya la ausencia no es ausencia
y podemos salir a cualquier parte.

The Grammar of Absence

for Miguel Gomes

I don't want to revisit that street
where the demolished houses
still stand.

Or read at this hour either
those poems of mine
I know I could not have written.

Is it useful to me finally
to revisit la rue de Turenne
if those ships I traveled in
never set sail?

The grammar of absence
parses voices so bitter
they imply something else always
than what we imagined.

Contact for me with the world
thus favors the conditional,
no believing in roots
or endings.

Best of all might be to see rain
falling on roofs without cease
while the street in sunlight goes ever drier.
It rains then but doesn't, or better,
absence is no longer absence
and we can leave for wherever.

Aquí otra vez

Aquí otra vez la rueda azul del cosmos
con estas acacias me anochece.
Un resto de luz tiembla en las hojas
y voces sin sonido
donde reitera el viento
su viejo ateísmo solitario.
Quedan dos o tres pensamientos dando vueltas
y al fondo de la sombra
algo que canta.

Creer o descreer no modifica
la persistencia de la rueda
siempre girante.
El canto de allá afuera
viene de tan lejos que casi ya no cabe
en un cuerpo pequeño y emplumado.
Y sin embargo, en esta hora,
si algo queda de Dios
se oye en los pájaros.

Here Again

Here again the blue wheel of cosmos
and these acacias shadow me over.
The remaining light trembles in leaves
and soundless voices
in which the wind repeats
its old lonely atheism.
Two or three thoughts circling still—
and in the depths of shadow
something that sings.

Believing or not believing won't alter
the wheel's perseverance, its
unceasing turning.
The song from out there
comes from so far it hardly fits
the small feathered body.
And yet at this hour
if something's left of God
we hear it in birds.

El último gallo

Había una vez un gallo ronco —el último,
el más solo de todos,
allá en las viejas horas de la tierra,
y aun íngrimo cantaba.
No supe nunca para qué, pero cantaba,
él y su sombra a pleno día,
él y los astros en las noches de aquel tiempo.
(Entre los tonos de sus ecos
se avivaba la luz de las estrellas.)

Había una vez el gallo que menciono,
el final de su especie,
con sus tonemas solitarios
de noche y día y en las silentes madrugadas.
Y dentro de ese gallo había algún otro
que cantaba su sueño
y así hasta el infinito,
multiplicando el grito en sus mil ecos,
allá en la tierra de aquel tiempo,
allá en mí mismo, pero a muchos siglos,
antes de yo nacer y de palparme,
antes de anochecerme, de ser sombra,
mucho antes.

Last Rooster

There was once a hoarse rooster—the last,
most lonely of all,
there in the old hours of the earth,
alone and yet it kept singing.
I never knew why but he sang,
he and his shadow at noon,
he and the stars of nights at that time.
(Among the tones of his echoes
the starlight grew brighter.)

There once was the rooster I mention,
last of its species
with its solitary tonemes
of night and day and soundless dawns.
And inside this bird was another
that sang its dream
and so on into infinity,
multiplying the cry in a thousand echoes,
there on earth at that time,
there in me, though many centuries
before I was born or felt myself so,
before I went dark, or was shadow,
so long before.

Heteronymic Works

From *El cuaderno de Blas Coll*

(1981, 1983, 2006)

PREFACIO

Tarde, muy tarde han llegado a mis manos los restos del Cuaderno de Blas Coll, cuyos fragmentos más legibles trato de recomponer en las anotaciones que transcribo. Su autor ya tenía más de veinte años de muerto al momento de mi hallazgo. He invertido cinco más en el intento de esclarecer la mayor parte de los pocos escritos que le sobreviven, pero sospecho que esta indagación minuciosa no dará cabal indicio de una labor tan heteróclita como la suya. Sigo ignorando todavía, pese a mis arduas pesquisas, si de verdad está enterrado en la pequeña aldea pesquera de Puerto Malo, junto al antiguo cementerio marino que el acoso de las aguas hizo demoler, o si, como es la suposición más verosímil, se embarcó en una nave de carga, ya amargado al final de sus años, y se fue a morir a otro lugar. Casi todos sus papeles se han perdido, tal vez porque la extrañeza que pudieron despertar (si acaso alguna despertaron) invitó a destruirlos por parecer inservibles. La mujer en cuya casa vivió desde que llegara a nuestras tierras, no sabía leer, y hace mucho que ha muerto. No estableció con ella, al parecer, otro vínculo que la vecindad de un pensionista solitario, afable aunque lejano, pero tan precaria amistad se cortó fatalmente, cuando ya del todo fiel a sus teorías, terminó sin ser comprendido por ella ni por nadie. He pasado largo tiempo en esta casa. Algunos de sus papeles han servido luego para decorar un tabique rústico, como es costumbre en el lugar, junto a pobres estampas desvaídas. No todo en ellos, por desgracia, puede descifrarse, y entre lo poco que reúno, albergo la duda de no haber conseguido la lectura más esclarecedora. Habría querido transcribir este cuaderno en la misma forma que soñó Blas Coll, pero he desechado el propósito más por falta de aptitud que por temor a no ser comprendido.

Los escasos hechos de su vida que he rastreado se mezclan con el añadido deformante de la leyenda. Fue conocido como tipógrafo rural. Queda probado, además, que derivara con el tiempo a una mudez voluntaria, porque ello lo aseveran los contados testigos que le sobreviven. Si hubiese dado al menos con el Diccionario privado que llegó a concluir, o con la adaptación de la Biblia y La Odisea, acortadas en cientos de páginas sin sacrificar una línea de sus textos originales, me sentiría bastante más seguro. He recorrido muchas veces el camino que va de su casa a la imprenta, ya demolida, evocando sus pasos ante el escarnio de algunos y la piedad de casi todos. Pienso a menudo en el orgullo de su soledad, semejante al hijo de Heráclito, porque también Blas Coll llegó a creer, quizá, que no sólo no nos bañamos dos veces en el mismo río, sino que jamás hemos palpado sus aguas, y concluyó por esto de igual modo, hablando desde lejos, sirviéndose de gesticulaciones extrañas.

[E.M.]

EXTRACTOS

Nuestra lengua, como todas las de origen románico, ha consolidado su estructura durante el ascenso del cristianismo; ha sido creada no sólo sobre las ruinas de la cultura greco-latina, de la que se aprovecha, sino que su movimiento parece establecerse para impedir en ella todo lo que posibilitó el idioma de Ovidio, de Catulo, de Anacreonte. No es, por tanto, una lengua de goce, sino de penitencia: le falta concisión porque al hablante, al "pecador," se le castiga con ella; carece de declinaciones porque desdeña el politeísmo . . .

∽

La palabra del hombre tiende en secreto a una extensión máxima de dos sílabas, aunque su ideal expresivo sea siempre la unidad monosilábica. Una sola sílaba traduce cabalmente el esfuerzo de un paso sobre la tierra. Se corresponde con la distancia imaginaria a que nos situamos de todo objeto, hecho o acción. Pero debemos conceder que se juzgue más natural servirse no sólo de un pie, sino de ambos, es decir, que se procure emplear el mayor movimiento posible sin repetición: sístole y diástole del corazón humano. Al nombrar una cosa con tres sílabas ya estamos añadiendo un paso de más que fatiga a la imaginación.

∽

Don Blas aseguraba que la oposición sujeto-predicado era el molino de viento que la imaginación tomaba por gigante. Decía que mejor llegaría a expresarse el que se guiara por el lenguaje de los pájaros, y fuese del sonido a la idea, y no de la idea al sonido siguiendo los recovecos tramposos de la lógica.

∽

Me río de los políticos que quieren ordenar las cosas de los hombres sin tocar su lenguaje. Tratan de ignorar adrede que la falacia de sus leyes es de índole lingüística más que jurídica.

∽

La palabra Dios en cualquier lengua tiende a ser monosilábica: su tiempo, su duración es el de un latido del corazón que la pronuncia. Un Dios bisílabo es posible, como sabemos, pero secretamente hospeda cierta creencia politeísta.

∾

Todo el proceso de siglos de lo que damos en llamar Edad Media se resume, mejor que nada, en la fatigante elaboración del artículo. Fue necesario un entrenamiento de inculpación colectiva y subsiguiente penitencia, gestado a lo largo de centurias tenebrosas, para imponer secretamente este peso, esta carga baldía como una cruz ante cada palabra de caso nominativo. Habría resultado absurdo, o poco menos, a cualquier súbdito del Imperio romano, concebir esta necesidad de anteponer una sobrecarga inútil a cada nombre. Si despertásemos alguna cautela en el común de la gente para suprimir el hábito de la articulación, o para denunciar su futilidad, estaríamos dando un buen paso hacia una lengua nueva. Esta sola iniciativa valdría para desencadenar muchas otras, que acercarían el habla al placer mucho más que al dolor.

∾

Es más difícil ser cristiano en alemán que en castellano, por ser aquélla una lengua declinable. ¿No estará allí, acaso, el secreto del panteísmo que recorre el alma germánica?

∾

Creo, tengo que creerlo a la vista de estos fragmentos que Don Blas perdió la razón apenas se adentró en la materialización de sus teorías. O tal vez, como muchos añaden, fue precisamente la falta de razón la que pudo llevarlo a una hipertrofia lingüística tan devastadora para sí mismo. Siento, así y todo, compasión por su locura, aunque se me haga por momentos borroso, lo confieso, lo que de noble haya en su empeño obstinado. Fue a su modo un suicida, pero se cuidó de crear esforzadamente un álgebra personal para escribirnos su última carta. Y tal vez esto me aclare el sentido de mi compasión: es que esa carta suya es toda su obra disparatada.

∾

La lógica sirve a la realidad tanto como la geometría a las nubes. De expresarse a través de formas rígidas y predeterminadas, qué poco encanto ofrecen a la contemplación las cambiantes formas de un nubario matinal.

∿

¿A dónde vamos con una lengua que, en estado de supremo peligro para el hablante, le impone decir: *s-o-c-o-r-r-o*? Cuando alguien así grita, mar adentro, se me antoja replicar desde aquí: ¡déjenlo que se ahogue!

∿

Toda frase debe reproducir en su construcción, tanto como sea posible, la forma de gravitación de los astros que conocemos. El sujeto debe rotar como el sol.

∿

Los refranes y decires anónimos, hermosos y sintéticos, son las botellas que arroja al mar cada idioma de tiempo en tiempo.

∿

No hay que confundir la lengua crucificante de la política cristiana con el alma de Jesús de Nazaret, aunque la Iglesia se empeñe en hacernos ver que ambas son una y la misma cosa. Muy poco queda de Cristo, como bien advirtió Nietzsche, en las representaciones que procuran apropiarse su doctrina, y absolutamente nada de su espíritu se refleja en esta lengua de cómitres.

∿

Hay quienes comentan su suicidio (del que no he logrado ninguna prueba cierta) como una hazaña estrambótica, al avanzar hacia el mar llevando en sus bolsillos todos los tipos de su imprenta para hundirse con ellos. Otros refieren su muerte en términos parecidos, pero agregan que sólo portaba consigo cuanto juzgaba superfluo para el uso cotidiano de los signos, lo cual, si calibramos bien su tentativa de expurgación, le habría bastado suficientemente para aniquilarse.

∿

En un viejo muro he podido leer un breve fragmento, seguramente anotado allí por él durante su primera época, que traducido a nuestra lengua aproximadamente diría: *La naturaleza es taquigráfica.*

༄

No creo que sea el hombre quien inventa su habla, como se admite comúnmente, sino las cosas y fenómenos naturales los que a través de éste se expresan. El lenguaje es el paisaje, y no a la inversa. No tengo a mano los medios para probar esto, pero de haber sido grabada la lengua de los indígenas que habitaron en Puerto Malo, dispondría ahora de mayor exactitud al recomendar los nuevos vocablos, puesto que una lengua es ante todo su lugar.

El idioma de los norteamericanos, por ejemplo, bien puede resultar algo rudo al oído de los británicos, pero sin duda esa rudeza es un paso en la evolución hacia su propia lengua. Un día, sin saberlo, hablarán como los árboles y los pájaros que los rodean, como los vientos en sus piedras milenarias. Con los años añadirán nuevos sonidos, desecharán otros, el viejo acento del *Mayflower* resultará cada vez más lejano. Toda su habla de hoy puede parecerle a algunos una extraña y fea oruga, pero de allí ha de salir la mariposa.

༄

La estructura de la oración debería de variar con el transcurso del día, para señalarnos del modo más preciso el registro del tiempo. No conviene hablar por la mañana del mismo modo en que lo hacemos por la noche.

༄

El pensamiento es el nudo de la idea. Y sin nudo no hay significación posible; por eso los dementes, que no logran atar ideas, nunca se expresan de verdad, aunque crean hacerlo. Al conversar con alguien tratamos de anudar nuestro pensamiento al del interlocutor, mediante formas convencionales y prácticas seculares en las cuales nos entrenamos como los marineros con sus cabos. "Atar cabos," reza el lugar común con precisión. Y los marineros avezados saben que hay muchos modos de anudar y que no siempre conviene dar más vueltas al cable de las que se precisan. Yo no he sido marino, aunque llevo años en esta bahía calurosa. Pero me he habituado a mirar las ideas como naves a las que es necesario atar del modo más sencillo y duradero posible.

Constituye una mutilación cruel, para decir lo menos, que enseñemos a los niños a reconocer las letras antes que las notas musicales. Por allí comienza, para los párvulos, la sorda tiranía de la abstracción, que les impide el inmediato conocimiento de la realidad. Al ronco clamor de los sapos o al más melodioso de los pájaros se antepone, con los años, el espúreo cepo del abecedario. Y nada digamos del mágico color de las vocales, ese vívido color de nuestra infancia, tan prontamente reprimido. Sólo Arthur Rimbaud pudo llegar a ser, como dicen los ingleses, Arthur Rainbow.

Hay quienes socarronamente aseguran que Blas Coll eligió su apellido por las dos eles finales, de las cuales creía servirse al modo de dos zancos para atravesar los cenagosos pantanos de Puerto Malo.

Convendría estar atentos al momento del próximo diluvio, cuando nos toque partir de nuevo en el Arca. Sobre todo, no hay que olvidar a las iguanas, nuestras míticas gorgonas, pues ellas también deben salvarse.

Siete son las vocales de la lengua perfecta, como siete los principales orificios del cuerpo humano.

Los deberes son cóncavos, los derechos convexos.

No sabemos nunca cuándo, al hablar, dejamos de hablar nosotros mismos y autónomamente por nosotros habla el lenguaje. Los poetas, mucho más próximos de las raíces de la lengua, se habitúan a reconocer este estado de autonomía al que suelen dar el nombre de inspiración. Saben reconocerse como bocas de gárgolas marinas en tanto sientan que por ellos pasa a veces un poco de los inabarcables murmullos del mar.

Escrito en una hoja de almendrón

Lo más hermoso del viento entre los árboles es que, a su paso, prefiera hablar sin ninguna consonante; que sólo se sirva de vocales azules. Por eso su eco pervive largo tiempo después que ha saludado a la madera.

∾

Escrito en una hoja de malanga

La materia reposa en la nada como el hielo en el agua.

∾

El Añalejo

Bajo el nombre del *Añalejo* se conservó por mucho tiempo en la imprenta de Blas Coll un cuaderno de formato grande, parecido al que emplean los tenedores de libros, probablemente un ejemplar sobrante de alguna tirada numerada, que adquirió un significativo valor entre quienes frecuentaban el taller del viejo tipógrafo. Ocurre que el grueso volumen tuvo un atractivo destino pues, en vez de inutilizársele como sucede en la tipografía con las piezas excedentes o defectuosas, en él anotó Blas Coll de su puño y letra ciertas frases más o menos ingeniosas y algún tiempo después tanto él como casi todos los colígrafos, al azar del momento y en distintas ocasiones, se dieron a la contagiosa tarea de enriquecer las páginas del *Añalejo*.

Puede inferirse que participaron en su escritura más de seis personas, a juzgar por las características grafológicas visibles en sus páginas. Constituyen en su mayoría meras ocurrencias, decires, sentencias, cuando no simples observaciones e ironías del momento. El nombre del volumen deriva de una palabra originalmente impresa en la carátula del referido cuaderno.

A continuación reproduzco una pequeña serie de estas apuntaciones, transcritas sin firma ni fecha, tal como aparecen copiadas, las cuales he extractado del conjunto. Vine a tener noticias del *Añalejo* gracias a la profesora Amelia de Rivas, estudiosa de la obra de los colígrafos, a quien pertenece el manuscrito original del cual he espigado la muestra que de seguida se consigna.

∽

La tierra no es redonda en todas partes de la misma manera.

∽

Las letras son de Dios, el alfabeto es nuestro.

∽

La sangre del azul también es roja.

∽

Perros que ladran sin convicción.

∽

En la mujer hay algo siempre que la asemeja a una orquesta. No es prudente aproximársele sin una batuta.

∾

Los pensamientos crecen como las uñas, sólo que a mucha mayor velocidad.

∾

Nuestro nada saber que es tan humano . . .

∾

Pobres cigarras, no saben que somos sordos.

∾

La publicidad es la religión del bufón.

∾

No trates de enseñar al gato a pisar más fuerte.

∾

No estaba loco del todo porque odiaba mucho.

∾

Cuando mi pobre hamaca se enferma, me quedo en casa a cuidarla.

∾

La luna es nuestra flor carnívora.

∾

El sapo que se traga un insecto puede tragarse una estrella entera.

∾

La poesía no es verdad ni mentira, es lo que diga su ritmo.

∾

Las ruedas del carro de la Historia son cuadradas.

∾

Quien no pueda nombrar el paraíso con una sola sílaba puede estar seguro de que no lo merece.

∾

Un pájaro que tomase conciencia—en medio de su canto—de lo que verdaderamente hace, ya no sería un pájaro, sino un Mozart.

∾

Los dioses son siempre muy poco explícitos.

∾

El silencio es una piedra que debemos pulir todos los días de nuestra vida.

∾

El Logos es un pájaro con las alas húmedas que toca a las puertas del aire.

From *The Notebook of Blas Coll*

(1981, 1983, 2006)

PREFACE

Late, very late, I happened upon the remnants of the Notebook of Blas Coll, the most legible fragments of which I attempt to transcribe in these notes. Its author had been dead more than twenty years when I discovered it. I have invested five more, hoping to clarify in large part the few writings that survive, though I suspect this meticulous investigation will fail to reflect truly a work as unorthodox as his. Much escapes me still, despite my arduous inquiries. Is he really buried in the fishing village of Puerto Malo, in that ancient seaside cemetery washed away by battering waves? Or, as the more likely story goes, did he board a cargo ship, bitter in his later years, and go off to die elsewhere? Nearly all his papers have been lost, perhaps because the surprise they aroused (if indeed they did) prompted someone to destroy them, thinking them useless. The woman in whose house he had lived from the start could not read, and died long ago. Apparently he had been merely a retired lodger to her, solitary, affable but distant—and yet the tenuous friendship between them inevitably ended when, true to his theories, he stopped being understood by her, or by anybody. I have spent a good deal of time in this house. Some of his papers were used later on, along with a few cheap faded pictures, to decorate a shabby partition, as is the custom here. Unfortunately, not all of these are decipherable, and given the handful I have gathered, I fear I have not rendered the most illuminating reading. I would have liked to transcribe the notebook in the form Blas Coll envisioned, but have given up trying, more for lack of ability than for fear of not being understood.

The scant facts of his life I have unearthed are intermixed with the added distortions of legend. He was known as a small-town printer. We know also that in time he became voluntarily mute; the few witnesses still living have said so. If I come across the private Dictionary he completed, or his adaptations of the Bible or *The Odyssey,* abridged by hundreds of pages without sacrificing a single line of the original texts, I would feel more confident. I have traveled the road that runs from his house to the now-demolished print shop again and again, retracing his footsteps, ridiculed by some and pitied by nearly all. I often imagine him in his proud solitude, like Heraclitus's son, because Blas Coll came to think, it would seem, that not only do we not bathe in the same river twice but also that we never touch its water—and thus he ended up likewise, speaking from far off, reduced to strange gesticulations.

[E.M.]

EXCERPTS

Our language, like all those of Romantic origin, was consolidated structurally during the rise of Christianity; not only was it built on the ruins of Greco-Latin culture, which it exploited, but its trajectory seemed designed to suppress all the possibility that Ovid, Catullus, and Anacreon offered. It is less a language of pleasure than of penance: it lacks conciseness because the speaker, the "sinner," is afflicted by it; it lacks declensions because it scorns polytheism . . .

∾

Human speech tends in essence toward a maximum length of two syllables, though its expressive ideal is always the monosyllabic unit. A single syllable translates precisely the pressure of one footstep on earth. It corresponds to the imaginary distance by which we situate ourselves relative to every object, fact, or action. Still, we cannot but admit it would be more natural to use not just one foot, but both—that is, to try to employ the best motion possible without repetition: the systole and diastole of the human heart. Name a thing with three syllables and we add an extra step that fatigues the imagination.

∾

Don Blas asserted that the subject-predicate opposition was a windmill that the imagination mistook for a giant. He said one would express oneself best guided by the language of birds, moving from sound to idea, not from idea to sound following the sinuous deceptions of logic.

∾

Politicians amuse me, trying as they do to orchestrate the affairs of mankind without understanding its language. They deliberately try to ignore the fact that fallacies in law are linguistic rather than legal.

∾

The word God in any language tends to be monosyllabic: its time, its duration is that of the heartbeat of the person who utters it. A bisyllabic God is possible, as we know—even while it secretly harbors a certain polytheist belief.

∾

One could sum up the interval of centuries we call the Middle Ages, for lack of a better term, as the tedious production of the article. Lessons in collective accusation and subsequent penitence were needed, gestated during the course of shadowy centuries to secretly impose this burden, this useless cross to bear, preceding every word in the nominative case. It would have been absurd, basically, for any subject of the Roman empire to conceive of the need to set such useless baggage before every noun. If we were to awaken in the common people a scruple to suppress the habit of using articles or to denounce their futility, we would be taking healthy steps toward a new language. This single initiative would serve to trigger others, each approaching the speech of pleasure rather than pain.

∾

It is harder to be Christian in German than in Spanish, given that it is a declinable language. Is this not perhaps the secret of the pantheism flowing in the Germanic soul?

∾

I believe, I have to believe, seeing these fragments, that Don Blas lost his mind as soon as he began fully realizing his theories. Or maybe (as some suggest) it was precisely such loss of reason that drove him to the linguistic hypertrophy that was so personally devastating. I do pity his madness, though just how noble his stubborn endeavor was is not clear to me, I admit. It was a form of suicide, yes—but also his way of creating, with great effort, a personal algebra with which he wrote his last letter. This may help explain my compassion: that letter of his sums up the whole of his ludicrous corpus.

∾

Reality needs logic like clouds need geometry. Rigid, predetermined forms of expression offer little magic to contemplating the shifting shapes of a cloudy morning.

∾

Where do we go with a language wherein, when faced with great danger, its speaker must say: *s-o-c-o-r-r-o?* When someone shouts thus, out to sea, I'd like to answer from here: let him drown!

Every clause must replicate in its construction, as closely as possible, the gravitational pull of the known stars. The subject must rotate like the sun.

Anonymous proverbs and sayings, synthetic and lovely, are the bottles each idiom now and then casts into the sea.

We must not confuse the crucifying language of Christian politics with the soul of Jesus of Nazareth, though the Church is committed to making us think the two are one and the same. Very little remains of Christ, as Nietzsche well noted, in the depictions the Church employs appropriating his doctrine, and nothing of his spirit is reflected in this language of tyrants.

There are some who describe his suicide (of which I have found no clear evidence) as an outlandish act of advancing into the sea, pockets laden with all his printer's type, and sinking. Others attribute his death in similar terms, but add that he bore with him only the symbols he deemed superfluous for everyday use—enough, actually, if we properly calibrate his attempt to expurgate symbols, to destroy him.

On an old wall I managed to decipher a short fragment, jotted there by Coll, certainly in his early phase, which, roughly translated to our language, reads: *Nature is shorthand.*

I do not think that man invents speech, as is commonly thought, but that things and natural phenomena express themselves through him. Language is landscape, not the inverse. I do not have at hand a means by which to test this, but if the language of the Indians once occupying Puerto Malo had been recorded and were at my disposal, I could be more precise in suggesting new vocabularies, given that language is above all a place.

The language of North Americans, for example, can indeed seem rough to the ears of the British, but this crudeness is no doubt a step in the evolution of their own language. One day without knowing it they will speak like the trees and birds that surround them, like the wind on thousand-year-old stones. In time they will add new sounds, reject others, the old accent of the *Mayflower* becoming more distant at each turn. To some their language as a whole today may seem a strange and ugly caterpillar, but it's from this that the butterfly will emerge.

∾

The structure of speech should vary over the course of the day, marking for us in the clearest way possible the passing of time. It is not useful to speak in the morning the way we do in the evening.

∾

The thought is the knot of the idea. And without a knot, meaning is not possible; the insane, therefore, who cannot quite rein in ideas, never truly communicate, though they think they do. Conversing with someone, we try to tie our thought to that of our interlocutor through the conventional forms and age-old practices we learn to master like sailors with bits of rope: to tie up loose ends, as they say. Seasoned sailors know there are many ways to tie knots, and know it's not good to wrap the rope around more times than necessary. I am no sailor, though I have spent years on this warm bay. I have grown accustomed to seeing ideas as ships to be tied up, though necessarily in the simplest, most enduring way possible.

∾

A cruel deformation it is, to say the least, that we teach children to recognize letters before musical notes. There and then begins, for infants, the deaf tyranny of abstraction, impeding their direct understanding of reality. Before the hoarse clamor of toads or more melodious noise of birds, they interpose, year upon year, the spurious trap of the alphabet. Not to mention the magic color of vowels, the lively color of our infancy, so quickly suppressed. Only Arthur Rimbaud could come to be, as the English say, Arthur Rainbow.

∾

There are those who slyly suggest that Blas Coll chose his surname for its double *l*'s, which he believed could be used as stilts for crossing the boggy swamps of Puerto Malo.

∾

It would be well to pay attention when the next flood comes, when we are called upon again to board the Ark. Above all, we must not forget the iguanas, our mythic Gorgons, for they also need saving.

∾

Seven are the vowels of the perfect language, corresponding to the seven principal orifices of the human body.

∾

Duties are concave; rights are convex.

∾

We never know when, in speaking, we ourselves stop speaking and language speaks autonomously through us. Poets, much closer to the roots of language, are used to recognizing this state of autonomy, which they tend to call inspiration. They come to feel like the mouths of marine rain-gutter gargoyles, noting traces of the endless oceanic murmurs that sometimes flow through them.

∾

Written on an Almond Leaf

The loveliest thing about wind in the trees is when, as it blows, it chooses to speak without consonants; it uses only blue vowels. Thus the echo remains, long after it has greeted the branch.

∾

Written on a Stem of Grass

Matter rests in the void like ice in water.

∾

The Almanac

Preserved for many years at Blas Coll's press was a large-format notebook called the *Almanac*, similar to those used in bookkeeping, probably an extra copy from a numbered print run, which those who frequented the shop of the old printer came to treasure. The thick volume had an auspicious fate, it turns out, because instead of discarding it in the usual way of defective or surplus pieces at presses, Blas Coll used it to jot down particular, more or less ingenious, phrases by hand, and so did nearly all of the *colígrafos* later on, at random moments and on different occasions, each contributing to the contagious labor of enriching the pages of the *Almanac*.

One can infer that more than six people participated in the writing, judging by the characteristics of the handwriting on its pages. It is composed in large part of witty remarks, sayings, and maxims, as well as idle observations and ironies of the day. The name of the volume derives from a word originally printed on the title page of the notebook in question.

I reproduce here a short sequence of these quips, transcribed without attribution or date, just as they were written, although extracted from the whole. I came to learn of the *Almanac* thanks to Professor Amelia de Rivas, scholar of the work of the *colígrafos*, who holds the original manuscript from which I have gleaned the following sample.

∾

The earth isn't round everywhere in the same way.

∾

Letters are God's, the alphabet our own.

∾

Blue blood is also red.

∾

Dogs barking halfheartedly.

∾

In woman there is always something like an orchestra. It's not prudent to approach her without a baton.

Thoughts grow like fingernails, only at much greater speed.

～

Our not knowing is so human . . .

～

Poor cicadas, they don't know we're deaf.

～

Advertising is the religion of the clown.

～

Don't try to teach the cat to tread harder.

～

He wasn't completely crazy because he hated much.

～

When my poor hammock is ailing I stay home to tend it.

～

The moon is our carnivorous flower.

～

The toad that swallows an insect can swallow an entire star.

～

Poetry isn't true or false; it's what its rhythm says it is.

～

The wheels of the train of History are square.

～

Anybody unable to name paradise in a single syllable can be sure he or she doesn't deserve it.

～

A bird conscious of what it truly does while it sings would not be a bird but a Mozart.

∽

The gods are never terribly clear.

∽

Silence is a stone we need to polish every day of our lives.

∽

The Word is a bird with damp wings knocking on doors of air.

∽

From *Guitarra del horizonte,* *por Sergio Sandoval* (1991)

PREFACIO

Entre quienes nos iniciábamos en el aprendizaje del oficio poético al promediar el siglo, allá en los añorados días de nuestra juventud, sin duda el menos conocido, pero también el más singular del grupo, fue el temerleño Sergio Sandoval. Sabíamos que había sido uno de quienes frecuentaron, como aprendices o contertulios, el taller tipográfico de Blas Coll, es decir, uno de los últimos colígrafos, como ellos mismos se llamaban, aunque no el más ortodoxo pese a la devoción que manifestaba por el desaparecido lingüista de Puerto Malo.

Las proposiciones artísticas a que se adhería lo apartaban radicalmente de las nuestras, como es de ver en el libro que ahora doy a la luz. Desde sus primeros pasos, mientras los demás nos reconocíamos atraídos por las líneas renovadoras de la lírica moderna, él asumía con inmodificable denuedo el culto de la forma más popular y sencilla, la copla anónima, que veneraba con entusiasmo casi místico. Consecuente con su propósito, cuanto queda de él es sólo un cuaderno de coplas, al pie de cada una de las cuales anotó una suerte de glosa íntima, a modo de complementaria recreación de su empeño lírico. De ese cuaderno, la presente muestra, que acompaño con esta primera noticia acerca de su vida y menester artístico.

Sergio Sandoval (1936–1969) nació en Temerla, una apacible y apartada aldea del Estado Yaracuy. Como varios de nosotros, se inició en el estudio del Derecho, aunque la acción política de los bandos que se hostigaban a diario terminase por alejarlo para siempre del ambiente universitario. Durante aquellos años en que el simple hecho de no optar por una de las formas de lucha despertaba un indicio sospechoso, él eligió la práctica solitaria de la no violencia, que por supuesto lo oponía a casi todos a la vez. No pudo reconocerse cerca de los necesitados, de los oprimidos por las castas poderosas, pero se resistía a reivindicar el odio militante como principio para modificar el mundo. Creo que el ideal de su prédica apuntaba a un cambio íntegro del hombre, al alumbramiento de una nueva conciencia, sin la cual, según su parecer, al cabo resurgirían bajo nuevas formas las tentaciones de dominio de unos hacia otros. Como un raro, esquivo y distante, Sandoval asumió la soledad de su vocación sin cuidarse de divulgar su propio trabajo. Tampoco se detuvo a confrontar con nosotros sus opiniones literarias. Se limitó a compartir, cuando lo hizo, como un compañero ocasional, una que otra velada de café en aquellos azarosos años. Pienso ahora que a sus ojos debimos de parecer inocentes diletantes, ilusionados por un arte indeciso y pasajero. Estoy seguro, además, de que a muchos de quienes lo trataron les resultará extraña la sola mención de su nombre entre los poetas del grupo. Nunca se tuvo por tal. El cultivo de la única forma que hizo suya, la copla octosilábica, acaso le indujo el deseo de permanecer anónimo, como si en ello identificara la aspiración predilecta del genuino poeta.

[E.M.]

EXTRACTOS

I

Se fue por este camino,
la vi perderse al final;
le hizo un nudo al horizonte
que no puedo desatar.

EL poema chino más común consta, al igual que nuestra copla, de cuatro versos. Su estructura tradicional reserva al primer verso la fase inicial de la composición; el segundo, por su parte, dialoga con el precedente y prolonga su contenido; el tercero introduce un elemento nuevo y desvía momentáneamente la atención; el cuarto debe resumir los primeros tres y cerrar la estrofa. Resulta difícil en nuestra lengua seguir el mismo procedimiento, tan propio del espíritu oriental, sin adulterar la forma fijada por la tradición. La copla se resuelve en una sola unidad concatenada, más cercana de la forma silogística. Sin embargo, algo nos dice que la tercera línea es a menudo el puesto de ruptura predominante, la cuerda de donde parte la flecha que más vulnera a la memoria. Así sucede en esta copla, que nada de chino tiene ni lo pretende, en cuyo tercer verso sobresale la imagen del nudo del horizonte como rastro del amor que se aleja. Los tres restantes renglones sólo parecen existir para justificar la tensión que la imagen comunica a todas las palabras.

II

Ando buscando un camino
que no se borre en el mar
para llevarte conmigo
donde los barcos no van.

El camino que corre por la voz de esta copla pretende ser tan claro como el agua, a la que debe su rumor, pero al revestirse de un deseo imposible se contagia de oscuridad, en este caso de la oscuridad insondable del mar. Con una y otra intención se relacionan las palabras, por eso resultan sencillas o complejas, según se las lea. La estrofa parece proponer un *koan,* aunque no se valga de interrogantes sino de expectativas. En efecto, quien busca un camino que en el mar no desaparezca busca el sonido de una sola mano, busca lo impensable, lo que acaso pueda iluminarnos. Por lo demás, bien se sabe que el sentimiento tiene zonas adonde las palabras, como los barcos de esta copla, nunca se acercan. Y allí arraiga casi siempre el sentido inefable de la verdadera canción.

VII

En la copa de una palma
que un ventarrón sacudía,
un pajarito cantaba
y el canto no se movía.

Con la palma en que se posa, hacia donde el viento lleve las ramas, se mueve el cuerpo del pájaro. Si a ella se aferra es porque tiene confianza en la raíz que la sostiene. Por fuerte que sea el ventarrón, la palma ha educado a sus hojas para resistirlo, aprovechando sus embates y moviéndose a su propio favor sin contrariarlo. Bajo el acoso de las ráfagas se agitan las ramas, la copa se cimbra, y todo el plumaje del pájaro se engrifa. Sólo el canto permanece inalterable, repitiendo su eterna melodía siempre nueva, y unido a una raíz más profunda que la de ningún árbol en la tierra.

IX

Cuerda larga y sin clavija
que suenas de monte a monte,
¡quién te tocara algún día,
guitarra del horizonte!

Entre todas las coplas que he compuesto, ésta acaso sea una de las que atesore más silencio. Siento en ella hacerse tenso el vacío que la circunda, como si la imposibilidad que nos evoca impusiera un silencio mayor para imaginar el sonido de la inalcanzable guitarra que nos dibuja el horizonte. ¿Qué hombre acostumbrado a la visión de la llanura no habrá soñado pulsarla alguna vez, bajo el cambiante espejismo de las tolvaneras? Es una cuerda larga que no tiene clavija, abierta a los cuatro rumbos de la soledad. A veces en el viento creemos oírla y nos gana el deseo de correr hasta ella y tocarla con nuestras propias manos.

La escribí una soleada mañana, andando por tierras de Barinas, adonde llegué acompañado de un ilustre baquiano de aquellos rumbos, mi fraternal amigo José Vicente Abreu, maestro en el conocimiento de la llanura, quien ha refrendado en mi ánimo la veneración por la copla como supremo arte de nuestro canto popular.

XV

La lluvia va preguntando,
calle abajo y calle arriba,
quién le cambia al tordo negro
su canto por unas migas.

De todos los pájaros, el único que sobrevive suelto en nuestras ciudades es el tordo negro, el *tordito,* cuyo negro plumaje, siempre más intenso en el macho, a veces se tornasola con tintes de un azul profundo. Es el único que al hombre disputa las calles sin que nadie se atreva a maltratarlo, como ocurre con otros de más llamativos colores que ya no se ven, salvo en algún remoto paraje. El *tordito* vuela de una acera a otra, no lo aturde el ruido de las fábricas ni el monóxido de los autos. Hace nido en cualquier árbol y su presencia resulta ahora tan urbana como el celaje de los taxis o el pregón de los buhoneros.

No he leído aún el bando municipal que disponga la protección de este pájaro amigo, ¡y cuánto lo merece! Sólo la lluvia parece velar a su favor y demandarnos las migas que tanto le debemos. ¿Qué sería de nuestra vida diaria sin el porte menudo y familiar de los *torditos?* Es el último canto libre que nos queda.

XX

Viejo cuaderno de coplas
al fondo de mi morral,
quien piense que te he mentido
que te abra de par en par.

De tanto andar conmigo, inseparable compañero, el viejo cuaderno donde anoto mis coplas desde hace tantos años ya luce gastado y amarillo. No he querido reemplazarlo todavía pues tiene muchas páginas útiles; además, ¿por qué iría a escribir en otro lo que en él aún puedo anotar? Bajo mi almohada, a veces, ha dormido conmigo; tiene las tachaduras que la vida ha ido intercalando entre sus líneas; mi letra corre por sus páginas como no sabría hacerlo por otras. Es, de todo lo mío, lo primero que trato de llevar adonde voy. Sólo escribo en él las coplas que, aquí y allá, mi corazón inventa; no pocas veces tacho, tratando de corregir lo que después verifico como un capricho momentáneo. En otras ocasiones la copla llega como dictada por el aire. Y en unas y otras encuentro escrita mi vida en un sucesivo milagro, tal como he querido aceptarla día tras día.

XXIX

En cada gota una letra
la lluvia deja caer;
ranita que estás cantando,
¿quién te ha enseñado a leer?

No sabría decir por qué la lluvia de esta copla vino a mí bajo una imagen alfabética. Tanto depende de una caminata lluviosa a la orilla de las ciénagas. El recio sonido de los goterones sobre la ropa y el sombrero nos llevan a su antojo. Puede que al comienzo uno se resista y apure el paso, queriendo evadirse del aguacero. Después el agua nos gana y, como los árboles, nos entregamos a su deleite.

La pequeña rana que aquí aparece lee y canta a la vez. Lee de oídas, puede decirse. La copla deja sin respuesta la pregunta final: ¿quién instruye a la rana sobre el silabario de la lluvia? El lector a quien le sean familiares las palabras de San Francisco de Asís bien puede responder. Es *sor'acqua,* la dulce hermana agua, capaz de enseñar la lectura a las ranas, y al hombre la piedad y el amor infinito.

XXXVI

En el país de las flores
donde es abril todo el año
me enamoré de una espina
para evitar desengaños.

Esta copla de ánimo ligero se me ocurrió al término de un viaje. No llegué al país de las flores que ella menciona pues tal país, si existe, el olvido debe de custodiarlo. La recojo ahora porque fue real el desengaño y alguna verdad guardan para mí sus palabras, aunque me reproche el haberla resuelto por la vía irónica del juego de sentidos. Raro es el versificador que alguna vez no se haya servido de estos efectos que muchas veces distraen el sentimiento de su intención profunda, prestándole un brillo pasajero. La copla pura tiene la voz transparente del agua que jamás ironiza, y se atiene a su verdad de gozo o de pena cuando nos dice su canción. El buen ojo de mi maestro coplista supo advertir la debilidad del efecto pues me hizo este amable reparo: "En el país de las flores debemos amar las flores, cualquiera sea la suerte que nos toque, o largarnos al país de las espinas."

XXXIX

Si tu belleza mañana
no la recuerda el espejo,
la recordarán mis ojos
porque mis ojos te vieron.

La promesa que se lee en esta copla, más que un voto de amor, es un grito contra el acoso del tiempo, uno de esos gritos que nos arrancan las horas cuando el encuentro de algún ser que amamos nos hace desear otra vida menos efímera. Si los espejos, fríos y olvidadizos, nada retienen, ¿quién guardará mañana la belleza que nos hizo sentir por ella misma tan avaro el paso del tiempo? Sólo los ojos del amante —dice la copla— pueden conservar el testimonio de la verdad que contemplaron. Lo demás es el eco mudo del grito, y el misterio indescifrable de no saber si tras la muerte volverá alguna vez la visión que nos acompañó sobre la tierra.

XLIII

Infierno de calle ajena,
camino de Dios te valga,
los carros pasan veloces
y los árboles se apartan.

Mi contrariada permanencia en la ciudad me ha predispuesto contra los autos, avivando en mí la convicción, ya un tanto tópica en nuestra hora, de que el automóvil y el hombre no pueden convivir juntos por mucho más tiempo. Un joven compañero de nuestro grupo me dio a leer hace poco una página sobre el tema, cuyo título rinde homenaje al ameno Fray Antonio de Guevara: *Menosprecio del auto y alabanza del tren.* No molestaré al lector intercalando aquí sus diatribas contra el automóvil, ese pernicioso artefacto de nuestro infierno contemporáneo. Voy a la copla: venía yo caminando por una grata vereda que hasta entonces desconocía, uno de esos secretos recodos que aún se ocultan intactos dentro de las ciudades modernas. De pronto el ruido me hizo percatarme de que la calle desembocaba en una ancha avenida llena de automovilistas desesperados. Cada sombra fugaz parecía vestirse con su furioso vehículo, al modo de una armadura medieval. ¿A dónde iban tan urgidos, como huyendo de sí mismos? Del bulto de sus sombras sólo quedaba un golpe de viento seco que sacudía a los árboles, apartándolos de la vía.

～

Por muchas razones el presente Decálogo constituye una página que hemos de tomar en cuenta a la hora de aproximarnos a la obra de Sergio Sandoval. No sólo fue ésta una de las pocas que publicó en *La gaceta de Puerto Malo,* sino que además se trata de la última suya allí reproducida, por cierto pocos meses antes de su muerte.

Apareció en un número dedicado al venidero fin de milenio y lo que ha de ser su repercusión en el imaginario colectivo. Algunos de los redactores insinuaban el término 'milenismo' como nombre de las tendencias artísticas que despuntaban, en vez de 'post vanguardia,' el nombre que a la sazón comenzaba a divulgarse. Otros argüían que 'milenismo' podría fácilmente confundirse con el milenarismo nacido alrededor del crucial año mil. A esto replicaban los primeros que 'post vanguardia,' aparte de ser una expresión de poca gracia, sonaba a post mortem. Unos y otros se tenían ya entonces, acaso debido al calor del lugar, por artistas finimilénicos.

La contribución de Sandoval se limitó a los diez principios que insertamos de seguidas, por lo demás un típico modo suyo de subrayar distanciamiento. Según los comentarios suscitados por su breve texto, a él le importaba mucho más que la discusión propuesta por *La gaceta* la necesidad de advertir el peligro que debe salvar la humanidad para atravesar el terrible desfiladero del siglo XXI y parte del XXII. Creía entrever en las postrimerías de éste último el inicio de una era más benéfica, de acentuado predominio espiritual, pero no encontraba nada fácil el acceso a ella. Sin duda por esto llamó a sus diez enunciados *Decálogo de sobrevida.*

Decálogo de sobrevida

    I.   No luches por ninguna patria, lengua ni raza en particular. Defiende al hombre planetario.

    II.   Ten un hijo solamente y cuídalo más que a ti mismo.

    III.   Desdeña el dinero, pero no te impongas la pobreza forzada.

    IV.   No prestes tu cuerpo ni tu voz a ninguna forma publicitaria.

    V.   No detestes demasiado a tu ciudad: construye un pedazo de campo a tu alrededor.

    VI.   No elogies a ningún hombre vivo o muerto por sus hazañas bélicas. La única batalla que cuenta es la de la imaginación.

    VII.   Trata a cada hombre como a tu superior en la escala sagrada, aunque no creas en una escala sagrada.

    VIII.   No te aísles. Habla con todos los hombres que puedas, el mayor tiempo que puedas.

    IX.   Busca a tu mujer en un pueblo distinto del tuyo.

    X.   Paga diariamente tu derecho a la vida con actos de bondad práctica.

From *Guitar of the Horizon,* by Sergio Sandoval (1991)

PREFACE

Among those of us who began our apprenticeship as poets mid-century, in those nostalgic days of our youth, the least recognized and most unusual in our group was surely Sergio Sandoval of Temerla. We knew he had frequented the print shop of Blas Coll as an apprentice or to attend literary gatherings—he was one of the last *coligrafos*, as they called themselves—though Sandoval himself was not terribly orthodox, despite his obvious devotion to the vanished linguist of Puerto Malo.

The artistic tenets to which he adhered departed radically from ours, as the volume I now bring to light will illustrate. Even very early on, while the rest of us were drawn to the innovative lines of the modern poem, he devoted himself with unstinting effort to that simplest, most popular form, the anonymous *copla*, which he venerated with almost mystical enthusiasm. Consistent with his purpose, what remains is a single notebook of *coplas*; at the foot of each we find an annotation by him, a kind of intimate gloss, a complementary re-creating of his poetic efforts. From that notebook comes the sample that follows, to which I add this first account of his life and artistic work.

Sergio Sandoval (1936–1969) was born in Temerla, a quiet, isolated village in the state of Yaracuy. Like any number of us, he began by studying law, but political acts by hostile factions wound up separating him forever from the university setting. Back then, when the mere fact of not opting for one form of struggle or another awakened suspicion, Sandoval chose the solitary practice of non-violence, which of course put him at odds with nearly everyone. He could not align himself truly with the needy, with those oppressed by the ruling class, nor could he uphold militant hatred as a way to change the world. The ideal his discourse proposes, I think, entails a complete change in mankind, the birth of new awareness; without this, he felt, new temptations would rise to lead us again to tyrannize others. Eccentric, elusive, and distant, Sandoval adopted a poet's seclusion, unconcerned about publicizing his work. Nor did he bother to meet with us to exchange aesthetic reflections. The most he did was share an evening at a café as an occasional companion, if that, back then in those turbulent years. In his eyes, I think, we must have seemed naïve dilettantes, deluded by a tentative and transient art. I am sure, also, that many who knew him would find it odd for his name to be listed among the group's poets. He never considered himself such. Maybe by cultivating the unique form he made his own, the octosyllabic stanza, he learned to love anonymity, as if to him this were the best way to aspire to the role of true poet.

[E.M.]

I

She left by this road,
I saw her disappear finally;
she made the horizon a knot
that I cannot untie.

The most common Chinese poem consists, like this *copla*, of four lines. Its traditional structure assigns to the first line the initial phase of the composition; the second, in its way, responds to the first and extends its content; the third introduces a new element and momentarily diverts attention; the fourth must sum up the first three and close the poem. It is difficult in our language to follow the same procedure, so characteristic of the Eastern spirit, and not adulterate the form fixed by tradition. The stanza is resolved in a single interlinked unity, closest in form to the syllogism. The third line is nonetheless the crucial point of rupture, we sense—the bowstring from which the arrow flies to most wound the mind. And so it happens in this stanza—which is not Chinese at all nor pretends to be—in which the image of the knot in the third line lingers like a vestige of love after love vanishes. The other three lines appear to exist only to justify the tension the image imparts to every last word.

II

I walk along seeking a road
that the sea won't erase
just so you will come with me
where the boats do not go.

The road flowing through the voice of this stanza tries to be clear as water, to which it owes its murmur, and yet imbuing itself with an impossible desire, it takes on tinges of darkness, in this case the bottomless dark of the sea. With one intent or another its words interact, and are finally complex or simple, depending on how they are read. The poem seems to offer a *koan,* though it employs expectations rather than questions. Indeed, whoever seeks a road that the sea won't dissolve seeks the sound of one hand clapping, seeks the unthinkable, that which may someday enlighten us. Still, one knows that emotions have zones wherein words, like the boats in the stanza, never approach. And it is there almost always that the ineffable sense of the true song is rooted.

VII

In the crown of a palm
a strong wind was shaking,
a small bird was singing
and the singing remains.

In the palm in which it has landed, while the wind blows the branches, the bird's body trembles. If it clings to the palm, it's because it believes deeply in the root which supports it. Hard as the wind blows, the palms fronds are trained to withstand; they make use of the onslaught, shaking unresistingly at the wind's whim. As gusts tear at the branches the crown sways; the bird's feathers all stand on end. Only its song stays unchanged, and though its melody repeats endlessly, it's still always new, tapping a root deeper than that of any tree on earth.

IX

Unending string, no peg for tuning,
sounding mountain to mountain,
if only one day I could play you,
guitar of the horizon!

Among all the *coplas* I have composed, this is one of those perhaps that holds most silence. I feel the emptiness surrounding it tighten, as if the impossibility it evokes imposed greater silence by imagining the sound of the intangible guitar that the horizon inscribes for us. Who accustomed to seeing the plains has not dreamed of strumming it in the wavering mirage of dust storms? It is one unending string, with no peg for tuning, open to the four directions of solitude. At times, thinking we hear it on the wind, we are overcome by the desire to dash up and play it with our own hands.

I wrote this one sunny morning, walking around Barinas, in the company of a distinguished guide from those parts, my dear friend José Vicente Abreu, expert in knowledge of the plains, who endorsed in my spirit a veneration for the *copla* as the highest art of our popular song.

The rain falling is asking,
up street and down
who'll trade the starling
some crumbs for its song.

Of all birds, the only one surviving uncaged in our cities is the starling, *el tordito,* the little blackbird, whose black plumage, always more intense in the male, takes on tints of deep blue at times. It's the only bird that confronts people on the streets—no one dares to mistreat it, unlike the more striking birds we do not see anymore, except in the most remote places. The starling flits from one sidewalk to the next, unfazed by the roar of factories or the fumes of cars. It makes its nest in whichever tree; it now seems as urban as the taxi's horn or the cries of vendors.

I have never read of any ordinance offering protection for this friendly bird—and how it deserves it! Only the rain seems to guard it, demanding of us the crumbs we owe. What would our daily lives be without the example of the tiny familiar *tordito*? Its song is the last free song that remains.

XX

Old notebook of coplas
in the depths of my backpack,
whoever believes I deceived you
should open you fully.

After so much traveling about with me, my inseparable companion, this old notebook in which for years I have set down my *coplas*, now looks wasted and yellowed. I have not wanted to replace it, given its many blank pages; besides, why would I write in another what I might jot down in this one? It has slept under my pillow at times; it holds corrections life has interspersed between lines; my writing flows in its pages as it could not in others. Of all that is mine it is the first thing I pack wherever I go. In it I write only the *coplas* my heart invents now and then; I cross things out often, hoping to correct what I decide later was a momentary caprice. At other times the *copla* arrives as if dictated by air. And in one or another I find my life written as a continuing miracle, exactly as I wanted to embrace it day after day.

From Guitarra del horizonte, por Sergio Sandoval   191

XXIX

In every drop the rain
lets a letter fall;
tiny frog who is singing,
who taught you to read?

I cannot say why the rain in this *copla* came to me as an alphabetical image. So much depends on a long rainy walk at the edge of the swamp. The roar of huge raindrops on clothes and hat transports us at its whim. We might resist at the outset and hurry along, hoping to escape the downpour. Later, the water conquers, and like the trees, we succumb to delight.

The little frog that appears here reads and sings simultaneously. It reads by ear, one might say. The *copla* leaves the final question unanswered: who instructed the frog in the spelling book of the rain? A reader familiar with the words of Saint Francis of Assisi might well answer. It is *sor'acqua,* sweet sister water, able to teach frogs to read, and teach mankind mercy and infinite love.

XXXVI

In the country of flowers
where it's April all year
I fell in love with a thorn
to not end up deceived.

This light-spirited *copla* came to me at the end of a journey. I did not visit the country of flowers it mentions; if such a country exists, it must be locked in obscurity. I offer the poem because the deception was real, and its words hold some truth for me, though I regret it comes through the irony of a play on meaning. Rare is the poet who has not made use of such effects at some point, which often distract feeling from its deeper intent, lending it a fleeting brilliance. The pure *copla* has the transparent voice of water; it is never ironic, and abides by its truth of joy or sadness in relating its song. My *copla* master with his sharp eye was wary of the weakness of its effect and offered me this friendly riposte: "In the country of flowers we must love flowers, be our luck as it may, or we hasten to the country of thorns."

From Guitarra del horizonte, por Sergio Sandoval   193

XXXIX

If the mirror doesn't recall
your beauty tomorrow
my eyes will recall you
because my eyes took you in.

More than a vow of love, the promise one finds in this *copla* is a cry against the onslaught of time, one of the cries the hours wrench from us when contact with a being we love makes us crave a life less ephemeral. If mirrors, forgetful and cold, retain nothing, who will keep the beauty tomorrow that for her sake made us so jealous of the passing of time? Only the eyes of the lover—the *copla* states—can retain the testimony of truth they contemplated. What's left is the silent echo of a cry, and the indecipherable mystery of not knowing if after death the vision we knew on earth will remain.

XLIII

Infernal alien street,
God-help-us highway,
cars are flying by quickly
and trees part to make way.

My ill-fated stay in the city has biased me against automobiles, stirring in me the conviction, already a cliché these days, that people and automobiles will not be able to live together much longer. A young member of our group recently gave me a piece to read on this subject, whose title pays homage to lively Brother Antonio de Guevara: *Contempt for the Car and Praise for the Train*. I will not annoy the reader by citing here his diatribes against the automobile, that pernicious artifact of our contemporary hell. But to return to the *copla*: I was walking along a pleasant alley I'd just discovered, one of those hidden lanes still found intact in modern cities. A roar warned me suddenly that the lane flowed into a wide avenue full of desperate motorists. Each fleeting ghost seemed to be dressed in its furious vehicle, in the manner of medieval armor. Where were they all heading so urgently, as if fleeing from themselves? Amidst the shadows only a blast of dry wind remained, shaking the trees, driving them out of the way.

For a number of reasons, the Decalogue that follows is essential to approaching the work of Sergio Sandoval. It was one of the few pieces he published in the *Puerto Malo Gazette*, and the last he published there—indeed just months before his death.

It appeared in an issue dedicated to the coming end of the millennium and what its impact would necessarily be on the collective imagination. Some of the newspaper's editors used the word "millennialism" to evoke certain burgeoning artistic tendencies, rather than "postmodern," the name that had begun circulating then. Others argued that "millennialism" could easily be confused with the millenarianism arising around that crucial thousandth year. To this, the first group replied that, apart from being a graceless expression, "postmodern" sounded like "postmortem." By then one or another of them considered themselves, thanks perhaps to the heat of the place, end-of-the-millennium artists.

Sandoval's contribution is merely a list of ten principles, appearing as follows, a not-unusual mode of his to emphasize distanciation. According to commentaries prompted by this brief piece, the discussion proposed by the *Gazette* was far less important to Sandoval than warning mankind about the danger it faced crossing the terrible threshold between the twenty-first and twenty-second centuries. Sandoval believed he could see in our current century's end the beginning of a more charitable era, predominantly spiritual, though he did not think getting there would be easy. No doubt for this reason he called his ten statements *Decalogue for Survival*.

Decalogue for Survival

I.   Don't fight for any country, language, or race in particular. Defend the planetary man.

II.   Have one child only, and care for that child more than for yourself.

III.   Disdain money, but don't take on poverty willingly.

IV.   Don't lend your body or voice to any form of publicity.

V.   Don't hate your city too much: build a bit of country around you.

VI.   Don't praise any person, living or dead, for warlike deeds. The only battle that counts is that of the imagination.

VII.   Treat every person as your superior on the spiritual scale, even if you do not believe in a spiritual scale.

VIII.   Don't isolate yourself. Converse with all the people you can, for as long as you can.

IX.   Seek out your wife in a village distant from yours.

X.   Pay daily your right to life by practicing acts of kindness.

Essays

From *La ventana oblicua* (1974)

LOS TERRORES DE CAER EN K

Confieso mis temores ante la letra K. Es la duodécima de nuestro alfabeto, la novena consonante, quizás la menos eficaz pero la más peligrosa. Los diccionarios voluminosos no le consagran más de tres páginas, casi todas apretujadas de palabras exóticas, impronunciables, accesorias. Podría eliminarse y confiar a la C dura, que ha heredado todo el esfuerzo de la Kappa griega, su antiguo trabajo. Podría culpársele de amparar el mayor número de neologismos y vocablos atragantados. Empero, su casi inutilidad no mengua un ápice el enigmático respeto con que siempre domina. Porque habla menos que sus hermanas, y siempre en lengua extraña, está más llena de silencio y es más significante la K.

Disimula sus poderes una geometría de líneas rectas, que integran una vertical y dos oblicuas, intersectadas por encima de su altura media. Reconozcamos su belleza angular, tan perfecta como la A o la Z. Más que éstas, parece acumular una suma máxima de tensiones. Su reposo está cargado de fuerza, no diferente del arco, y con la perfección acoplada de una saeta. Mis temores, sin embargo, proceden de su identificación antropomorfa. La K semeja, con una precisión sutil, las extremidades de un hombre en marcha. Es un hombre que siempre camina, no sé hacia dónde ni por qué, con la erosión esquelética de una escultura de Giacometti. Sus huesos han tomado el grosor de su cuerpo en una liviandad metálica. La K soporta, por eso, grandes marchas. Pero es una marcha desolada, por landas cenicientas, baldías y, no sabría tampoco por qué, antaño pobladas, florecientes. La K recorre esa extensión en silencio, interfiere en un volumen escaso de palabras, no se la comprende ni espera ser comprendida. Padece un exilio superior al de la X o la Y. Si se la observa, se sabe que desdeña la locuacidad de la M, el torpe tableteo de la T. La K tal vez por esto no se detiene. Medita quizás el viejo aforismo taoísta: —el que sabe, no habla; el que habla, no sabe.

La K esgrime su altivez para ocultar su desamparo. Y su desamparo cae en evidencia. Nuestro temor no impide una tácita conmiseración. La K no representa peligro en ella misma; sabemos que el arco por sí sólo no se dispara. Los peligros están afuera y la rodean; por eso la evitamos y sentimos terror de su presencia. Son los terrores de caer en K. Porque K, desde cierto tiempo, no es en Occidente una simple letra, la convención gráfica de un componente de significados; es, más bien, un significante, una zona maldita, azarosa, amenazadora: K. Veamos por qué.

"Seguramente se había calumniado a K —dice la primera línea de *El Proceso*— pues, sin haber hecho nada malo, fue detenido una mañana." Tan breves frases, tan simples como absurdas, proponen menos un juego a la imaginación que una vidente alusión de extremado pavor. Pasamos las páginas para seguir una extraña mitología de la culpa que, a través de un engranaje perfectamente montado, concluye con la eliminación, sin razones reales o aparentes, de K. El condenado es muerto de manos de un verdugo oportuno con un puñal, que bien pudo ser un *kama*, "puñal circasiano de hoja muy ancha," o un *kangiar*, "puñal grande, a modo de machete," o un *klebán*, "especie de puñal corto javanés" (citas del Larousse). La suposición puede suplir la identificación del arma, aunque no el sitio en donde fue enterrada —el corazón—, ni la frase final del condenado: "como un perro, dijo, y era como si la vergüenza debiera sobrevivirle."

Kafka desdibujó una situación de condena sin causa, de ejecutoria sin palmos de lógica. K se había atado a un deber ser cotidianamente normal, incapaz de quebrantarle su integridad *de juris*. ¿Qué hizo K para caer en K? A esa pregunta Kafka no responde, y es de creer que escribe su libro para averiguarlo, ya que, según se sabe, no para publicarlo. ¿Era Kafka el mismo K, como se ha insinuado? Kafka temía llegar a ser el propio K, como cada uno de nosotros lo teme hoy en cualquier punto de la Tierra. De nada vale la objeción de Marta Robert de que Kafka, al publicar su obra, hubiese dado un nombre al personaje. Porque ese nombre no existe, y, simbólicamente, toda impensable hora de inculpación absurda en nuestro tiempo es K.

La condición de K se presenta, de común, montada sobre tres elementos: dos en relación directa y uno, el inculpado, sin conexión lógica y, por ello, factor de cuasi comicidad en la novela, y de angustia y temor en la vida real. Basta que, por un azar, encarnemos este tercer elemento para que hayamos caído en territorio de K y nadie pueda ya salvarnos. En *El Proceso,* esta condición se articula así: la sociedad (primer elemento) y el siempre inaccesible tribunal (segundo elemento), atrapan a K. La novela gana su fuerza de la ausencia de causalidad posible entre la víctima y el sumario. Años después, el esquema, ya no novelado sino terríficamente vivo, se presenta para el pueblo judío. Los campos de concentración exterminan a millones de hombres en la inocente condición de K.

Veamos que en *El Proceso,* el exterminio pudo ser lento, tramado, postergado y, en cierto modo, en Auschwitz lo fue. Pero también puede ser súbito, atronador, fulminante: la mañana del seis de agosto de 1945, en Hiroshima, y días después en Nagasaki, ciento cincuenta mil hombres sucumbieron bajo la atmósfera pestilencial de K.

La condición de K la esquematiza una total inocencia ante el ajusticiamiento, la indefensión del condenado, el azar de la circunstancia y el estupor con que el hombre constata la fragilidad de los valores morales, únicos a partir de los cuales es posible la vida.

La fatalidad de K repite a diario su aleatorio percance. Hace poco el conde Karl Von Spreti, Embajador alemán en Guatemala, pereció en la arácnida zona de K. Ajeno a una situación que se sirve de su vida como objeto, padece la estupidez de un azar que lo conecta a una pugnacidad de la cual es extraño. Desde estos umbrales temerosos debe ser releído *El Proceso.* Puede, incluso, inventarse un nombre judío o japonés o alemán: la condición de K posee en todas partes la misma identidad cruel, amenazante.

No se confunde con el riesgo moral o espiritual del héroe que desafía, por un sistema de ideas, el mecanismo inquisidor de su época, aunque su martirologio se torne igualmente brutal (Sócrates, Cristo, Galileo): es la pura inocencia atada a una mutilación sin causa.

Así puedo explicarme el temor que padezco ante la letra K. La miro cruzar en su mutismo la calle donde vivo. Tiene el aire lamentoso de un solo de flauta fúnebre. En sus huesos, palpo la corrosión atómica que Giacometti transmutaba a sus bronces. La saludo lejano y hago cuanto puedo por esquivarla. No es una letra, sino una condición, un espectro.

From *Indirect Views* (1974)

FEAR OF FALLING IN K

I am afraid of the letter K, I admit. It is the twelfth letter of our alphabet, and the ninth consonant, perhaps the least effective and yet the most dangerous. Voluminous dictionaries do not devote more than three pages to it, pages crammed mostly with exotic words, foreign in origin, unpronounceable, accessory. One might eliminate it and entrust its former function to the hard C, which has inherited all the vigor of the Greek *kappa*. K can be blamed for harboring the greatest number of neologisms, not to mention words one could choke on. Its near uselessness, however, does not diminish one iota of the enigmatic respect it always commands. Because it speaks less than its cohorts and always speaks in a strange tongue, K is more rich in silence, and more significant.

Concealing its power is its geometry of straight lines, which includes one vertical and two diagonal lines, all intersecting at the vertical midpoint. We can acknowledge its angular beauty, as perfect as that of A or Z. More than these two, it seems to embody a wide range of tensions. Its repose is imbued with force, not unlike a bow perfectly joined to an arrow. My fear, however, comes from an anthropomorphic association. With uncanny precision, K looks like the limbs of a person in motion. It is a person forever walking, I do not know where or why, melted and skeletal as a sculpture by Giacometti. Its body is mere bones worn down to metallic lightness. K thus endures long marches. But each is a desolate march, through wild ashen wastelands, lands once populated, flourishing (though I cannot say why). K travels the expanse in silence, emitting its sparse handful of words, neither understanding nor hoping to be understood. It suffers an exile superior to that of X or Y. If you notice, you will see it hates the loquaciousness of M, the clumsy clatter of T. For this reason, perhaps, K never stops. Maybe it ponders the old Taoist saying: he who knows doesn't speak; he who speaks doesn't know.

K wields its pride to conceal its helplessness. And its helplessness is fully evident. Our fear does not preclude tacit commiseration. K does not represent danger in itself; we know that the bow will not discharge on its own. The dangers lie beyond and surround it; therefore we avoid it and feel terror in its presence. Such is the fear of falling in K. Because for some time, in the West, K has not been a mere letter, a graphic convention in a compound of meaning. It is a signifier, rather, a place accursed, hazardous, menacing: K. Why is this so? one wonders.

"Someone must have been telling lies about K"—reads the first sentence in *The Trial*—"since without having done anything wrong he was arrested one morning." Such directness, simple as it is absurd, seems less a trick of the imagination than the graphic rendering of pure fear. Page by page we are drawn into a strange mythology of guilt which, thanks to its flawlessly orchestrated machinations, ends with the elimination, without real or apparent reason, of K. The condemned dies at the hands of an opportunistic executioner equipped with a dagger, which could well be a *kama,* "a Caucasian dagger with an extra-wide blade," or a *kangiar,* "a large dagger, like a machete," or a *klebán,* "a type of short Javanese dagger" (quoted from Larousse). One might guess at which it is, but not the place it was buried—the heart, which we know, along with the last words of the condemned: "'Like a dog!' he said; it was as if the shame of it must outlive him."

Kafka makes ambiguous a situation of condemnation without cause, of final judgment uncomprehended by logic. K is bound by an obligation to be routinely normal, incapable of violating his integrity *de juris.* What did K do to end up falling in K? Kafka does not answer this question; one wonders if he wrote his book to find out, since he did not intend, as we know, to publish it. Was Kafka this very K, as some have insinuated? Kafka was afraid of becoming K himself in the end, as afraid as each of the rest of us is everywhere else in the world. Marthe Robert's claim is not valid—that

Kafka, had he published the book, would have provided a name for his character. Because the name does not exist. And symbolically, every unthinkable hour of absurd accusation in our own age is K.

The condition of K usually presents itself based on three elements, two directly interrelated and another (the accused) lacking logical connection and therefore an element of quasi-humor in the novel, and of distress and fear in real life. If by any accident we embody this third element, we have already fallen in K territory and nothing can save us. In *The Trial* this condition articulates itself thus: society (first element) and the always inaccessible tribunal (second element) ensnare K. The novel gathers its force from the absence of causality existing between victim and indictment. Years later—not yet novelized but terrifyingly vivid—the plot turns up for the Jews. Concentration camps exterminate thousands of people in the innocent condition of K.

We see in *The Trial* that extermination can be slow, calculated, drawn out, and in a certain way in Auschwitz it was. But it can also be sudden, thunderous, and devastating: the morning of August 6, 1945, in Hiroshima, and days later in Nagasaki, one hundred fifty thousand persons fell victim to the pestilential atmosphere of K.

The condition of K is schematized as complete innocence before execution, the indefensibility of the condemned, the whim of circumstance, and the indifference with which people confirm the fragility of moral values, those that make life truly possible.

K's bad fortune recurs daily with its random mishaps. Not long ago Count Karl von Spreti, German ambassador to Guatemala, died in the arachnoid region of K. Not only was his life used in this case as an object of barter, he fell victim to the idiocy arising from a coincidence connecting him, an outsider, to a kind of bizarre aggression. From these fearful thresholds *The Trial* must be reread. It can take on Jewish names, even, or Japanese, or German: the condition of K everywhere holds the same cruel, menacing identity.

That identity should not be confused with the moral or spiritual risk of the hero who challenges the inquisition mechanism of his age through a system of ideas, and whose list of martyrs seems indeed equally brutal (Socrates, Christ, Galileo): this is pure innocence tied to destruction without cause.

Only thus can I explain the fear I suffer facing the letter K. I see it silently cross the street I live on. It has the lamenting air of a solo played by a funereal flute. In its bones I sense the atomic corrosion that Giacometti transmuted in his bronzes. I greet it from afar and I do all I can to avoid it. It is not a letter but a condition, a ghost.

From *El taller blanco* (1983, 1996)

POESÍA EN UN TIEMPO SIN POESÍA

Uno de los aforismos de Nicolás Gómez Dávila publicados en el número 211 de la revista bogotana *Eco,* reza literalmente: "Primera mitad del siglo XVIII, segunda mitad del siglo XX, los dos medios siglos más hueros de poesía en muchos siglos." La forma elusiva y lapidaria, propia de la escritura aforística, sin duda dispensa al autor de la incomodidad de los detalles, tan necesarios a la hora de esclarecernos su pensamiento y de examinar la rotundidad de un juicio semejante. La sentencia acusa, sin embargo, el trazo de una meditada convicción, lo cual la releva de cualquier sospecha de efectismo. Y tiene sobre todo el raro atractivo de declarar un parecer opuesto al común panegírico de la lírica contemporánea, aventurando una reprobación tan franca como demoledora.

El aforismo, apenas leído, suscita por lo menos tres reparos en el ánimo de un lector medianamente atento. El primero tiene que ver con el lapso a que en parte se ciñe su condenatoria, el de la segunda mitad de nuestro siglo, de la cual faltan dos décadas para que finalice y de cierto varias otras para juzgar con alguna objetividad su perspectiva. No habiendo concluido aún la otra mitad de la presente centuria, el juicio corre el riesgo de encarnar una predicción antes que una exacta comprobación de los hechos. Un segundo reparo nace de lo indeterminado del campo que examina, al punto que no sabemos si se refiere sólo a nuestra lengua o a todas las lenguas de occidente. Traído al ámbito de la lírica castellana, no deja de ser oportuno revisarlo. Por último, la sentencia divide tajantemente la primera y segunda mitad de nuestro siglo, siendo que, al menos en poesía tal división resulta inoperante. Negando la última parte, se niega tácitamente la primera, en la cual se hallan muchas de sus raíces teóricas y cuyas exploraciones en notable medida se prolongan hasta nuestros días.

Los reparos no le restan al fragmento el aire sugestivo que siempre despiertan las negaciones absolutas. Su declaración delata, como dije, una convicción que es sin duda el producto de estimaciones comparativas entre la poesía de hoy y la de las épocas pasadas. Hay que decir, además, que el reclamo no carece de filiación. Hugo Friedrich, por ejemplo, para citar a un renombrado estudioso de la lírica moderna, confiesa que pese a su cabal comprensión de la poesía contemporánea, se siente en mejor compañía con Goethe y los clásicos antiguos, que con Paul Valéry y T. S. Eliot.

El radicalismo de Gómez Dávila quizá procura contrarrestar otro reiterado con no poca frecuencia: el que trata de desvincular el arte del presente de toda relación con el pasado, imponiendo una visión lineal que erróneamente se ve corroborada en los avances del campo científico. Su reproche viene a tener por blanco principal la tendencia que Octavio Paz ha llamado la *posvanguardia*, cuya aparición tentativamente se sitúa hacia 1945, es decir, al término de la primera mitad de nuestro siglo. Pero, admitiendo como válido el distingo, ¿no es demasiado temprano para sopesar sus aportes cancelando las esperanzas de su evolución futura? Paz vuelve una y otra vez sobre el fin del "tiempo lineal," y es llamativa su advertencia de que en nuestra hora algo termina y algo nace. La estética del cambio constante, que marcó la primera vanguardia y acentuó el carácter histórico del poema, parece ahora quedar a un lado. La nueva lírica se abre más allá, en otro tiempo y frente a otras circunstancias. Esto lo lleva a preguntarse en forma conclusiva: "¿Fin del arte y de la poesía? No, fin de la era moderna y con ella de la idea de arte moderno" (*Los hijos del limo*). Ya no somos, pues, modernos, al menos en el sentido en que lo fueron Neruda, Bandeira, Eliot. ¿Qué somos? El título de una antología reciente de jóvenes españoles parece responder no sin humor a esta pregunta: *Poetas poscontemporáneos*. Dios los oiga.

Pero, volviendo a la sentencia que nos ocupa, ¿cuáles serían los síntomas de la lírica moderna que nos precisan su desventaja respecto de épocas anteriores? Es aquí donde, más que de poesía propiamente, conviene hablar de la condición del poeta en el tiempo presente y de las posibilidades a su alcance para, tanto como pueda, *purificar las palabras de la tribu*. Tal vez nunca antes, como ahora, fueron más unánimes las declaraciones sobre la dificultad creadora por parte de los propios poetas. El tema constituye ya un tópico fácil de constatar a partir de los simbolistas y quizás antes, el cual no ha cesado de acentuarse hasta nuestros días. "Es difícil ser poeta en una época industrial," anotó a comienzos de siglo Herbert Read. Como crítico enterado y poeta él mismo, bien sabía lo que decía. Y lo sabía sobre todo por pertenecer a una de las generaciones a las que correspondió trazar el saldo de la revolución industrial inglesa, que tantas y tan notorias alteraciones introdujo en el mundo. Las citas al respecto podemos multiplicarlas, entresacándolas de muy diversas lenguas y períodos, sin que difieran mucho en su intención unas de otras. Anotemos, así y todo, una más, ésta debida al gran poeta italiano Giuseppe Ungaretti: "Yo me pregunto: ¿existe todavía la posibilidad de un lenguaje poético? Hoy el tiempo parece ser tan veloz que ya no existe posibilidad de relación entre tiempo y espacio, que ya no existe duración, es decir, que ya no existe la posibilidad de la contemplación y, por consiguiente, de expresión de la poesía" (*Vida de un hombre,* Monte Ávila Editores). Observemos que el pesimismo de ambas opiniones coincide en reprobar las mutaciones de la sensibilidad aparejadas por los cambios técnicos. La era industrial, para Read, y el tiempo veloz y hostil, para Ungaretti, configuran un mismo desarraigo, cuya exploración ha atraído por cierto la atención de pensadores notables. Muchas páginas de Heidegger, para nombrar uno de los más eminentes, reiteran a la luz de la reflexión filosófica un parecer bastante similar al de los propios poetas.

El tema, nada inédito por lo demás, demanda mayor espacio que el de una simple nota y una competencia más calificada. Pretendo ahora, no obstante, representármelo en una realidad concreta que puede, en mi opinión, objetivamente resumirlo. Nada nuevo se añade con decir que esa realidad se localiza del modo más notorio en la pérdida de la ciudad como centro espiritual donde halla su arraigo privilegiado la poesía. Convendrá siempre, pese a todo, repetirlo. Lo que nombramos con la palabra ciudad significa algo completamente distinto antes y después de la aparición del motor, al punto que tal vez no resulte apropiado lingüísticamente homologar, si deseamos llamar las cosas por sus nombres, la urbe moderna con la apacible comarca de otras edades.

Hoy podemos advertir, tras la pérdida de ese espacio, de qué modo resulta imprescindible la relación del hombre y la ciudad para explicarnos las obras que nos legaron los artistas del pasado. Cada poema, cada obra de arte, encarna un diálogo secreto, a menudo amoroso, con las calles y las casas, las tradiciones y los mitos de ese poema mayor que en ella se fundamenta. El París de Baudelaire, la Alejandría de Cavafy, la Lisboa de los cuatro Pessoa, se nos tornan inseparables de sus logros artísticos en una medida tal que el destierro hubiese necesariamente supuesto su silencio definitivo. No hablo, por cierto, del destierro físico, siempre posible de sobrellevarse, pese a la crueldad que reviste, sin que se mutile el diálogo con ese espacio que, al fin y al cabo, se sabe existente, aunque prohibido, en alguna parte. El verdadero destierro, el desarraigo absoluto, comienza con la certeza de que ese lugar ya ha sido abolido para siempre, de que hoy somos, en una proporción desconocida para otras épocas y sólo ahora comprobable, *hombres sin ciudades.* En las urbes de nuestro tiempo, rectas y grises, ya no es posible la contemplación, como se lamenta Ungaretti. Y no basta con el deseo de alejarnos en busca de otra más en armonía con los requerimientos humanos, porque, aeropuerto tras aeropuerto, sus líneas se nos repiten idénticas dondequiera que lleguemos, con su prisa feroz y sus hervores mecánicos.

El poeta aparece así como el arquitecto por excelencia que reproduce a su modo la geometría espiritual de ese plano mayor donde halla lugar la vida común. Se sabe responsable de cada palabra como de cada casa y cada puente. La escala de sus equivalencias no se sirve de las leyes aritméticas para lograr su exactitud, pero la correspondencia de palabra y espacio hace ilegible la una sin lo otro. El sueño del libro absoluto de Mallarmé, ¿no es acaso el canto de cisne de esa última tentativa por retener lo que ya en su tiempo empezaba a desvanecerse? Y cuando el viejo Yeats, años más tarde confesaba: "Siento un gran deseo de crear forma," ¿a cuál forma perimida buscaba restituir si no a la que cobraba vida en la ciudad que alcanzó a ver?

El medio siglo más huero de poesía en tantos siglos, de que habla Gómez Dávila, se me aparece así como el más huero en espacio vital para la poesía. Me inclino a creer que no por ello la posteridad dejará de encontrar en las mejores voces de nuestra hora muchas palabras dignas de memoria. A la postre, lo más excitante del futuro es que no podemos suponerle benevolencia. "Todo porvenir es brutal," dice la institutriz de la novela *Otra vuelta de tuerca.* Pero cualquiera sea el parecer venidero acerca del arte de nuestro tiempo, será de todos modos innegable que cuanto se pudo salvar de la palabra fue mediante una lucha más ardua, aceptando un destino de expósitos.

Hoy sabemos que hemos llegado no sólo después de los dioses, como se ha repetido, sino también después de las ciudades. No es improbable que unos y otras retornen un día, pero celebrarlos ahora, para adular al futuro, sería cometer imperdonable falsedad. "El poeta —es de nuevo Herbert Read quien lo dice— tiene todos los privilegios, menos el de mentir."

From *The White Workshop* (1983, 1996)

POETRY IN A TIME WITHOUT POETRY

An aphorism published by Nicolás Gómez Dávila appearing recently in the Colombian journal *Eco* states to the letter: "First half of the eighteenth, second half of the twentieth, the two half centuries most devoid of poetry in many centuries." Elusive and dogmatic, aphoristic writing characteristically exempts an author from the inconvenience of details, so necessary to elucidating thought and to fully examining such a judgment. The maxim I cite reveals, nonetheless, traces of measured conviction, which absolves it of any hint of theatricality. Above all, it offers an opinion oddly and charmingly opposite to the kind of panegyric typically directed at contemporary poetry, and ventures a reprobation as frank as it is devastating.

Further considered, the statement raises three issues, if not more, for the moderately attentive reader. The first involves the error underlying, in part, Gómez Dávila's condemnation, concerning as it does the second half of our century, which is two decades away from concluding—and which will certainly (even when concluded) require various decades more to determine its place with any degree of objectivity. Immersed still in the latter part the century, the judgment runs the risk of embodying a prediction rather than clearly testing the facts. Second, given the indefiniteness of what he examines, one wonders if Gómez Dávila indicts poems in Spanish only or those in all Western languages. Focusing on the genre of poetry in Spanish, the judgment is worthy of review. Finally, the maxim divides our century categorically in two, despite the fact that (at least as far as poetry goes) such divisions are not really functional. To deny the latter half is to tacitly deny the first, where we find many of its theoretical roots, and whose explorations in poetry continue to a remarkable degree to this day.

Such issues do not detract from the provocative nature of the passage overall, ignite as it must with its wholesale dismissal. As a declaration, it betrays, I repeat, a conviction doubtless based on assessments comparing the poetry of today with that of past epochs. The complaint is not without adherents, I might add. Hugo Friedrich, for example—to cite a well-known scholar of modern verse—confesses that despite his wide understanding of contemporary poetry he finds himself in better company with Goethe and the classical ancients than with Paul Valéry and T. S. Eliot.

Gómez Dávila's radical stance intends perhaps to counteract another one, not infrequently reiterated: one hoping to dissociate the art of the present from all relation to the past, erroneously adopting the linear vision we see corroborated by advances in science. The main target of his re-proach is a tendency Octavio Paz has called *postmodernism,* whose appear-ance Paz tentatively locates around 1945--which is to say at the end of the first half of our century. Even if we did admit the distinction to be valid, we'd have to ask ourselves this: isn't it too soon to weigh its contribution and foreclose hope for future evolution? Paz returns again and again to the end of "linear time"; his suggestion that something has ended and some-thing new has begun is indeed striking. The aesthetic of perpetual change, which defined the first postmodern movement, stressing the historical na-ture of the poem, now no longer holds sway. The new poetry takes off be-yond, in another time, facing different circumstances. Which leads Paz to consciously wonder: "The end of art and of poetry? No, the end of the modern era, and with it the idea of modern art" (*Children of the Mire).* We are no longer, then, modern—at least in the sense that Neruda, Bandeira, and Eliot were. What are we? The title of a recent anthology of young Span-ish poets seems to answer, not without humor, the question: *Postcontem-porary Poets.* May God hear them.

But to return to the maxim in question: which aspects of the modern poem fare poorly in comparison to earlier epochs? Better here to consider the condition of the poet in the present day, rather than poetry per se, as well as the poet's capacity for *purifying the words of the tribe* however he or she might. Perhaps never more so than the present have declarations been as unanimous regarding creative difficulties on the part of poets themselves. The subject is well-rehearsed—arising with the Symbolists, if not before—and continues to be underscored in our time. "It is almost impossible to be a poet in an industrial age," Herbert Read wrote at the century's start. An informed critic and a poet to boot, Read knew well whereof he spoke. He knew, above all, by belonging to one of the generations entrusted with the task of sifting the results of the English industrial revolution, the numerous and obvious changes it introduced in the world. We could pile on more citations here, drawing from diverse languages and periods, without seeing much variation in purpose from one to another. Let us nevertheless point out one last, this by the great Italian poet Giuseppe Ungaretti: "I ask myself: does the possibility of a poetic language still exist? Today time seems to move so quickly, the possibility of a relation between time and space no longer exists, duration no longer exists, which is to say that the possibility of contemplation no longer exists—nor the possibility, consequently, of poetic expression" *(Vida de un hombre,* Monte Ávila Editores). The pessimism of both views, one may observe, similarly condemns mutations in sensibility tied to technical changes. For Read, the industrial era, and for Ungaretti, fleeting, hostile time—both constitute upheaval, the exploration of which has, to be sure, attracted the attention of prominent thinkers. Many pages in Heidegger, to name one of the most eminent, reiterate in the light of philosophy an opinion very like that of the poets.

The subject, familiar as it is, requires more space than this essay affords, and a more qualified assessment. For the moment, however, let me illuminate things in a way that might sum it up objectively. One adds nothing new by observing the problem to stem most visibly from the loss of the city as spiritual center, where poetry traditionally found its support. Even so, it bears repeating. What we designate with the word "city" means something completely different before and after the arrival of the engine, to such a degree that it does not seem fitting to linguistically equate—if we want to call things by their names—the modern metropolis with the peaceful burg of earlier times.

After the loss of such a space, it is now clear to us how essential the relation between individual and city is in explaining works that poets of the past have left us. Every poem, every work of art, embodies a secret dialogue, often romantic, with the streets and houses, the traditions and myths of that greater poem in which it is rooted. Baudelaire's Paris, Cavafy's Alexandria, and for the four Pessoas, Lisbon—each is inseparable from his artistic achievement to such a degree that exile would have necessarily meant definitive silence. I am not referring of course to the physical exile people must cope with, however cruel it may be, for such people are not cut off from dialogue with that space which in the end still exists, one understands, somewhere, even if forbidden. True exile, utter upheaval, begins with the certainty that that place has been wiped out forever, and with the recognition that we are today, in a proportion unknown to other epochs and only now verifiable, *men without cities*. In the rigid and gray metropolises of our time, contemplation is no longer possible, as Ungaretti laments. We might wish to move off in search of another, more in harmony with human needs, but that is not enough, because, airport after airport, its outlines are repeated identically wherever we land, along with its fierce bustle and mechanical noise.

The poet seems much like the architect par excellence who replicates in his way the spiritual geometry of that great plane where common life occurs. He knows he is responsible for each word, the way the architect is for each house and each bridge. The equivalence scale here does not rely on the laws of arithmetic for its exactitude, but the correspondence between word and space becomes illegible when one lacks the other. Doesn't Mallarmé's dream of the absolute book seem the swan song of that last effort to preserve what had already begun to disappear in his time? And when the aged Yeats confessed, years later, "I feel about and in me an impulse to create form," which obsolete form did he seek to restore if not that which emerged in the city he lived to see?

The half century most devoid of poetry in many centuries, to which Gómez Dávila refers, seems to me to be the most devoid of space for poetry. I am inclined to think that if for no other reason than this, posterity will find in the best voices of our day many words worthy of memory. Ultimately, what is most provocative about the future is that we cannot presume it will be benevolent. "All futures are rough," the governess says in *The Turn of the Screw*. Whatever the future opinion of our present art may be, it will be undeniable that whatever was salvaged of the word came by means of a struggle more arduous than any, one consigned to the fate of orphans. We know today we have not only arrived after the gods, as has often been said, but after cities as well. It is not unlikely that one or another will return one day, but to celebrate them now, to flatter the future, would be to commit an unforgivable falsehood. "The poet"—to quote Herbert Read again—"holds all privileges, except that of lying."

EL TALLER BLANCO

Quienes en nuestros días se sienten atraídos por el aprendizaje de la escritura poética, pese a tantos impedimentos que procuran disuadirlos, no sabemos si para bien o para mal, pueden al fin y al cabo encaminar su vocación a través de un taller de poesía. El experimento es novedoso entre nosotros, pero cuenta, como en muchas otras partes, con un manifiesto número de defensores y detractores. La tentativa, sin embargo, aunque opera de forma más o menos idéntica, esto es, congregando a un guía y a una seleccionada docena de participantes, puede proporcionar resultados tan dispares como los mismos grupos que la integran. Depende en mucho de la formación y sensibilidad de los concurrentes, y sobre todo del clima fraterno y cordial que a través de la práctica llegue a establecerse. Lograr desde el inicio que cada uno distinga su voz en el coro, que no perciba en el guía más que a un persuasivo interlocutor, en vez de un conductor hegemónico, constituye sin duda un buen punto de partida. El hábito de la discusión fecunda, los estímulos al trabajo, el respeto mutuo y todo lo que, para usar una expresión de Matthew Arnold, podríamos llamar "la urbanidad literaria," se seguirá naturalmente de ello solo.

No desestimo, por mi parte, la conveniencia de los talleres, aunque me sienta secretamente escéptico respecto de sus alcances. Alimento el prejuicio, algo romántico, es verdad, de que la poesía como todo arte es una pasión solitaria. Una multitud, como advierte sagazmente Simone Weil, no puede ni siquiera sumar; el hombre precisa abstraerse en soledad para ejecutar esta simple operación. Por esto quizá el título puesto por Schönberg a su *Memorias* se me antoja uno de los más apropiados para resumir las peripecias de una vida consagrada al arte, a cualquier arte: *Cómo volverse solitario.* Sólo en la soledad alcanzamos a vislumbrar la parte de nosotros que es intransferible, y acaso ésta sea la única que paradójicamente merece comunicarse a los otros.

Sé que muchos replicarán que en poesía, amén de los dones innatos, cuenta un lado artesanal, propiamente técnico, común también a las demás artes tanto como a las modestas labores de orfebres. Son los llamados secretos del oficio, cuyo dominio es en cierta medida comunicable. No faltará, por otra parte, quien me recuerde el conocido apotegma de la Lautréamont: *la poesía debe ser hecha por todos.* El acervo del folklore parece confirmar el triunfo de esta contribución múltiple y anónima; según ella, las palabras se van puliendo al rodar entre los hombres, como las piedras de un río, y las que perviven resultan a la postre las más estimadas por el alma colectiva. Todo ello es verdad, con tal que no olvidemos que en cada instante de este proceso ha existido un hombre real, que nunca fueron varios, por innombrado que lo creamos. Sí, la poesía debe ser hecha por todos, pero fatalmente escrita por uno solo.

En cambio, cuanto corresponde a los procedimientos artesanales, a los secretos de hechura, a toda esa vasta zona que con sumo ingenio analiza R. G. Collingwood en su libro *Los principios del arte,* me parece que es éste el campo verdaderamente propicio al cual la gente del taller puede consagrarse. Puesto que escribimos en nuestra lengua, es en ella principalmente, vale decir en las creaciones que conforman su tradición, donde averiguaremos el *cómo* de su íntimo gobierno; del *qué* y del *cuándo* bien podremos aprender no sólo en la nuestra, sino en cuantas lleguemos a conocer.

La palabra *taller* tiene, según el *Diccionario de la Real Academia*, dos acepciones, una concreta y otra figurada. La primera se refiere al lugar en que se trabaja una obra de manos. La segunda habla de la escuela o seminario de ciencias donde concurren muchos a la común enseñanza. El taller de poesía tiene de una y de otra. Lo es en sentido real y figurado a la vez. Hay obra de mano como también participación en el común aprendizaje. Tal como existen hoy por hoy, yo y quienes cuentan más o menos mi edad no los conocimos. No tuvimos la dicha o desdicha de reunirnos para iniciarnos en el mester de poesía. ¿Dónde, pues, fuimos a aprenderlo? Otros responderán de acuerdo con sus personales derivaciones. En cuanto a mí, he dicho que no asistí a ningún lugar donde ganarme la experiencia del oficio. Así al menos, porque lo creía, lo he repetido. Quiero rectificar ahora este vano aserto pues no había reparado en que, siendo niño, muy niño, asistí intensamente a uno. Estuve mucho tiempo en el taller blanco.

Era éste un taller de verdad, como es verdad el pan nuestro de cada día. Mi padre había aprendido de muchacho el oficio de panadero. Se inició, como cualquier aprendiz, barriendo y cargando canastos, y llegó a ser con los años maestro de cuadra, hasta poseer más tarde su propia panadería, el taller que cobijó buena parte de mi infancia. No sé cómo pude antes olvidar lo que debo para mi arte y para mi vida a aquella cuadra, a aquellos hombres que, noche a noche, ritualmente, se congregaban ante los largos mesones a hacer el pan. Hablo de una vieja panadería, como ya no existen, de una amplia casa lo bastante grande para amontonar leña, almacenar cientos de sacos de harina y disponer los rectos tablones donde la masa toma cuerpo lentamente durante la noche antes del horneo. Son los seculares procedimientos casi medievales, más lentos y complicados que los actuales, pero más llenos de presencias míticas. El sentido del progreso redujo ese taller a un pequeño cubículo de aparatos eléctricos en que la tarea se simplifica mediante empleos mecanizados. Ya no son necesarias las carretadas de leña con su envolvente fragancia resinosa, ni la harina se apila en numerosos cuartos de almacenaje. ¿Para qué? El horno, en vez de una abovedada cámara de rojizos ladrillos, es ahora un cuadrado metálico de alto voltaje. Me pregunto, ¿podrá un muchacho de hoy aprender algo para su poesía en este enmurado cuchitril? No sé. En el taller blanco tal vez quedó fijado para mí uno de esos ámbitos míticos que Bachelard ha recreado al analizar *la poética del espacio*. La harina es la sustancia esencial que en mi memoria resguarda aquellos años. Su blancura lo contagiaba todo: las pestañas, las manos, el pelo, pero también las cosas, los gestos, las palabras. Nuestra casa se erguía como un iglú, la morada esquimal, bajo densas nevadas. Por eso, cuando años más tarde contemplé por vez primera en París la apacible nieve que caía, no mostré el asombro de un hombre de los trópicos. A esa vieja amiga ya la conocía. Sentí apenas una vaga curiosidad por verificar al tacto su suave presencia.

Hablo de un aprendizaje poético real, de técnicas que aún empleo en mis noches de trabajo, pues no deseo metaforizar adrede un simple recuerdo. Esto mismo que digo, *mis noches,* vienen de allí. Nocturna era la faena de los panaderos como nocturna es la mía, habituado desde siempre a las altas horas sosegadas que nos recompensan del bochorno de la canícula. Como ellos me he acostumbrado a la extrañeza de la afanosa vigilia mientras a nuestro redor todas las gentes duermen. Y en lo profundo de la noche lo blanco es doblemente blanco. No falta la luna en los muros, sobre la leña, las mesas, las gorras de los operarios. ¡Los doctos y sabios operarios! Hay algo de quirófano, de silencio en las pisadas y de celeridad en los movimientos. Es nada menos que el pan lo que silenciosamente se fabrica, el pan que reclamarán al alba para llevarlo a los hospitales, los colegios, los cuarteles, las casas. ¿Qué labor comparte tanta responsabilidad? ¿No es la misma preocupación de la poesía?

El horno, que todo lo apura, rojea en su fragua espoleando a quienes trabajan. Los panes, una vez amasados, son cubiertos con un lienzo y dispuestos en largos estantes como peces dormidos, hasta que alcanzan el punto en que deben hornearse. ¿Cuántas veces, al guardar el primer borrador de un poema para revisarlo después, no he sentido que lo cubro yo mismo con un lienzo para decidir más tarde su suerte? Y nada he dicho de aquellos jornaleros, serenos y graves, encallecidos, con su mitología de arrabal, de aguardiente pobre. ¿Debo buscar lo sagrado más lejos en mi vida, pintar la humana pureza con otro rostro? Cristo podía convertir las piedras en panes, por eso estuvo más cerca de la carpintería, ese hermoso taller de distinto color. Para estos hombres, que no me hablaron nunca de religión, acaso porque eran demasiado religiosos, Cristo estaba en la humildad de la harina y en la rojez del fuego que a medianoche comenzaba a arder.

Del taller blanco me traje el sentido de devoción a la existencia que tantas veces comprobé en esos maestros de la nocturnidad. La atención responsable a la hechura de las cosas, la fraternidad que contagiaba un destino común, en fin, la búsqueda de una sabiduría cordial que no nos induzca a mentirnos demasiado. ¿Cuántas veces, mirando los libros alineados a mi frente, no he evocado la hilera de tablones llenos de pan? ¿Puede una palabra llegar a la página con mayor cuidado, con más íntima atención que la puesta por ellos en sus productos? Daría cualquier cosa por aproximarme alguna vez a la perfecta ejecutoria de sus faenas nocturnas. Al taller blanco debo éstas y muchas otras enseñanzas de que me valgo cuando encaro la escritura de un texto.

El pan y las palabras se juntan en mi imaginación sacralizados por una misma persistencia. De noche, al acordarme ante la página, percibo en mi lámpara un halo de aquella antigua blancura que jamás me abandona. Ya no veo, es verdad, a los panaderos ni oigo de cerca sus pláticas fraternas; en vez de leños ardidos me rodean centelleantes líneas de neón; el canto de los gallos se ha trocado en ululantes sirenas y ruidos de taxis. La furia de la ciudad nueva aventó lejos las cosas y el tiempo del taller blanco. Y sin embargo, en mí pervive el ritual de sus noches. En cada palabra que escribo compruebo la prolongación del desvelo que congregaba a aquellos humildes artesanos.

Tal vez, de no haber asistido a sus cotidianas veladas, de no inmiscuirme en las hondas ceremonias de sus labores, habría de todos modos buscado cauce a mi a afán de poesía. El grito de Merlín me habría tentado siempre a seguir su rastro en el bosque. Sin embargo, no puedo imaginar dónde, si no allí, habría aprendido mi palabra a reconocerse en la devoción sagrada de la vida. Anoto esta última línea y escucho el crepitar de la leña, veo la humareda que se propaga, los icónicos rostros que van y vienen por la cuadra, la harina que minuciosamente recubre la memoria del taller blanco.

THE WHITE WORKSHOP

These days, anybody attracted to the craft of poetry—despite numerous discouraging obstacles, for good or ill—can set out on the path of that vocation by joining a poetry workshop. The experience is new for us here, and as elsewhere, counts a perceptible number of defenders and detractors. While functioning everywhere in more or less the same manner (a dozen chosen participants gathering around a poet-guide), the workshop can produce results as disparate as the students it includes. Much depends on the training and sensitivity of the individual participants, and above all, on a helpful, congenial climate gradually developing in practice. That each student distinguishes his or her own voice in the chorus, and that each sees the guide as a persuasive interlocutor, not a hegemonic dictator; these are surely important points of departure. Habits of fertile discussion, stimuli to work, mutual respect, and what we might call (to borrow a term from Matthew Arnold) "literary urbanity"—all of this arises naturally from such an environment.

I do not underestimate the usefulness of workshops, though I admit I am secretly skeptical about their results. I cherish the prejudice, however romantic, that like any art, poetry is a solitary passion. A crowd cannot add things together, as Simone Weil wisely suggests; a person must withdraw into solitude to perform this basic operation. For this reason the title given by Schoenberg to his *Memoirs* seems one of the most appropriate for summing up the vicissitudes of a life devoted to art: "How One Becomes Lonely." Only in isolation can we attain a glimpse of that part of ourselves which is immutable—and that part, paradoxically, may be the only part worth communicating to others.

I know many would argue that, beyond innate ability, poetry relies to some extent on craftsmanship, on strict technicality, as common in the other arts as in the modest labors of goldsmiths. Such are the so-called secrets of the trade, whose mastery is communicable to a certain degree. Even so, one would do well to remember Lautréamont's famous maxim: *poetry must be made by all.* The great richness of folklore seems to confirm the triumph of this prolific and anonymous contribution; like stones in a river, words grow polished rolling from person to person, and the words that survive in the end tend to be those most valued by the collective soul. All this is true, as long as we do not forget that at every step in the process a real person existed, that it was never a group, nameless as we believe him or her to be. Yes, poetry must be made for all—but inevitably it is written by one alone.

It is in the realm of artistic method, however—in secrets of the trade, that vast area R. G. Collingwood so deftly examines in his book *The Principles of Art*—that individuals in a workshop can most usefully devote themselves. Since we write in our native language, it is mainly in that language (in the works that make up its tradition, that is) that we investigate the *how* of its inner mechanisms; we can learn the *what* and *when* sufficiently not only in our own language but in whichever others we may acquire.

According to the *Diccionario de la Real Academia,* the word "workshop" has two meanings, one concrete and the other figurative. The first refers to a place in which an object is crafted by hand. The second signifies a class or learning seminar in which a number of people meet for common instruction. A poetry workshop is both—it is a workshop in the literal as well as figurative sense. Work is crafted there manually, even as there is participation in a common apprenticeship. Like others roughly my age, I did not experience workshops like the ones existing today. We did not have the fortune or misfortune to gather together for initiation into the poetry trade. Where, then, did we go to learn? Others will respond with tales about their own artistic births. I never studied anywhere to gain experience in writing, as I have said. At least that is what I used to repeat, because

I believed it. I would like now to correct this faulty pronouncement. When I was a very young child, I did in fact participate intensely in one. I spent a great deal of time in a white workshop.

This was a real workshop, as real as our daily bread. My father had learned the baker's trade as a boy. He began, like any apprentice, by sweeping and carrying baskets; in time he became a master baker and later owned his own bakery, that workshop occupying so much of my youth. I don't know how I could have forgotten all I owe that bakery for my art and my life, what I owe those men who congregated at the great tables, night after night, for the ritual of making bread. An old-fashioned bakery, this was, the kind that no longer exists, in a dwelling spacious enough to pile firewood in, to store hundreds of bags of flour, and to arrange the long trays where the dough slowly swelled each night before baking. Ancient, almost medieval methods, these, slower and more complicated than those of today, and more filled, too, with mythic presence. Progress has reduced this workshop to a small cell containing electric appliances, the task simplified by mechanical means. No need now for cartloads of firewood, with its enveloping fragrance of resin, nor for flour, piled high in the various storerooms. What for? The oven, rather than an arched cavern of reddish bricks, is now a box of high-voltage steel. Could a boy today, I wonder, absorb something for his art in this walled-in hovel? I don't know. Perhaps the white workshop has endured in my mind as one of those mythic environments, like those depicted by Bachelard and explored in *The Poetics of Space*. Flour is the essential substance keeping those years in my memory. Its whiteness blanketed everything: eyelashes, hands, and hair, as well as objects, gestures, words. Our house stood like an igloo, an Eskimo's home, under layers of snow. Thus, years later in Paris, when I first gazed on snow gently falling, I was not amazed, not the way a person from the tropics typically is. I knew that old friend already. I felt only a vague curiosity to confirm its softness by touching it.

I am speaking of an actual poetic apprenticeship, of techniques I still use in my nights of work—I don't want to make a simple memory a metaphor intentionally. The nights I refer to, *my nights,* began there. The bakers' work was nocturnal, as mine is nocturnal, long accustomed to the tranquil late hours that offset the heat of sultry late-summer days. Like them, I have gotten used to the oddness of the diligent vigil while everyone else all around is asleep. And in the depths of night, what is white is doubly white.

Moonlight glows on the walls, tables, firewood, on the workers' caps. The wise, knowing workers! There is something of an operating room here, the quiet steps and quick movements. It is bread, no less, that they silently make, bread that will be demanded at dawn to take to hospitals, schools, barracks, and homes. What other work involves such responsibility? Isn't poetry's preoccupation the same?

The oven, which purifies all, reddens all who work there with its enlivening fire. Once they are kneaded, the loaves of dough are covered with a cloth and placed like sleeping fish on long shelves until they reach the point when they can be baked. How many times have I felt, setting aside the first draft of a poem for future revision, that I'm covering it with a cloth to decide its fate later? And I have said nothing of the workers, calloused and solemn and calm, with their tales of the barrio and bad aguardiente. Why look elsewhere in my life for what is sacred, paint human purity in some other guise? Christ could turn stones to bread, which is why he was inclined toward carpentry, that beautiful workshop of a different color. For those men, too religious, perhaps, to ever speak to me of religion, Christ appeared in humble flour and in the red of the fire that began burning at midnight.

The white workshop instilled in me the sense of devotion to being that I witnessed so often in those masters of the nocturnal. A careful attention to the making of things, the camaraderie that a common objective provides, and that search for congenial wisdom, finally, that doesn't allow us to flatter ourselves too much. How often, looking at the books lined up before me, have I thought of those trays lined up full of bread? Can a word reach a page with more care, with more intimate attention, than what those men paid to their loaves? I would give anything to come close even once to the perfect execution of their nightly work. The white workshop has taught me this and much more, lessons I apply each time I begin writing.

Bread and words conjoin in my mind, made sacred by mutual perseverance. At night, finding myself facing a page, I see a halo of white around my lamp that never forsakes me. True, I don't see the bakers now, nor do I hear their fraternal chatter nearby; instead of burning wood, tubes of blazing neon surround me; the song of the roosters has been replaced by wailing sirens and the roar of taxis. The modern city's fury has swept away the white workshop's objects and hours and days. And yet its nightly ritual persists in me. With each word I write I find the vigil prolonged, the vigil that held those humble craftsmen together.

If I hadn't attended those regular vigils, if I hadn't immersed myself in profound ceremonies of labor, I'd still have found a way, I suppose, to channel my hunger for poetry. Merlin's cry would always have tempted me to follow that trail into the woods. Still, I can't imagine where, if not there, I might have learned my means for expressing sacred devotion to living. Even as I write these last words, I hear firewood crackle, I see the cloud of smoke swell and iconic faces come and go in the heat while flour coats the memory of the workshop completely in white.

Notes to the Selected Works

Pages noted refer to original/translation

POEMS

20/21   *Mayo* / May   The original versions of most of the poems in *Élegos* went untitled. Anthologizing poems from this volume later on, Montejo added titles and punctuation. I am following his lead, therefore, by opting to title and punctuate here. The titles of all poems in Spanish have been regularized in terms of capitalization. The original titles were capitalized differently in many cases, volume by volume and edition by edition.

44/46   *Sala de parto* / Delivery Room   Public hospitals in many parts of Latin America feature large special clinics set aside for baby deliveries and for those attending expectant mothers. Whole families sometimes congregate in such waiting rooms, or *salas*. All parties, in this sense, are "expecting."

48/49   *Letra profunda* / Letra Profunda   Because "Deep Letter" or "Profound Letter" seems less than euphonious in English, and because *profunda* retains the Latin connection to "fundament" (with its association to the body) I have chosen to leave this poem's title as is—untranslated.

58/59   *Terredad* / Terredad   Peter Boyle translates this Montejo neologism as "earthdom." Renderings ranging from "earthiness" to "earth-ity" have come into my hearing informally. My choice to leave the word in its original form, while less than totally satisfying, is meant to suggest the deeper drift of Montejo's coinage: the transient if eternal fullness that all creatures—human, animal, vegetable, or mineral—embody.

68/69   *Los hombres del país Orinoco* / Men from Orinoco   The Orinoco is one of the world's longest rivers and cuts Venezuela roughly in half. South of the river lies the state of Bolívar, one of the country's largest, wildest, and least habited regions. The term "Orinoco" here refers to the region, rather than to the river itself.

94/95   *alternan una S, y una R (¡con diéresis!)* / S and R alternate (in dieresis!)   "Dieresis" (*diéresis*) signifies both the separating of two vowel sounds (dividing a single syllable in two) and the division occurring in a line of poetry when coinciding with the end of a foot, or a word (thereby creating a pause). The poem graphically renders the second sense of the term.

100/101   *Honor al asno* / Honor the Ass   The word "*asno*" carries with it an air of refinement in Spanish that its counterpart in English ("ass") has lost, sadly. Even so, "donkey" or "burro" seem less fitting as possibilities. Robert Graves honored the word and animal in his 1951 translation of Apuleius; I hope to continue to honor them here.

112/113   *El Ávila me salve* / May the Ávila save me   The Ávila is a highly visible mountain north of Caracas separating the northern reaches of the city from the sea.

126/127   *Só a dor e as estrêlas são universais*   Translated, the poem's epigraph reads: "Only pain and the stars are universal."

134/135   *Holan, el checo, afilaba la espuela de su gallo* / Holan the Czech sharpened his rooster's spur   Vladimír Holan (1905–1980) was a poet and Nobel nominee known for his somber take on the world and for his abstruseness. He left the Catholic Church to join the Communist Party but left the party after the Communist takeover. His books include *Blouznivý vějíř, Triumf smrti,* and *Vanutí.* He is best known in English for his postwar works, including a longer poem, "Noc s Hamletem" ("A Night with Hamlet," 1964). He lived isolated and destitute in his later years, on the island of Kampa in Prague.

HETERONYMIC WORKS

149/160   *El cuaderno de Blas Coll* / *The Notebook of Blas Coll*   Montejo published *The Notebook of Blas Coll* in at least three different versions over the course of five printings, altering or expanding the text. I draw here from two different printed versions: one from 1983 and one from 2006. In some cases I have chosen earlier versions over later, if and when the earlier seemed better suited to English. I include only the first part of Montejo's preface.

155/166   *como bocas de gárgolas marinas* / like the mouths of marine rain-gutter gargoyles   "*Gárgolas marinas*" are stone figures (often in the shape of lions or dolphins) that serve as spouts for certain rain gutters; the figures often seem to spit water.

157/167   *El Añalejo / The Almanac*   "*Añalejo*" is an obscure, outdated word, unfamiliar even to readers of Spanish, signifying a liturgical calendar. The Spanish word evokes both "annual" and "yearbook," not to mention the poet's surname.

170/184   *la copla anónima /* the anonymous *copla*   Given the *copla's* significance in Montejo's culture, and given the fact that neither the word nor experience have equivalents in English, I have opted to leave it in Spanish. As with the preface to *Blas Coll,* I include only the first part of Montejo's preface to *Guitarra.*

181/195   *Menosprecio del auto y alabanza del tren /* Contempt for the Car and Praise for the Train   Translated, Antonio de Guevara's original title is "Contempt for the Court and Praise of the Village" (*Menosprecio de corte y alabanza de aldea,* Valladolid, 1539).

ESSAYS

203/206   *el conde Karl Von Spreti ... pereció en la arácnida zona de K /* Count Karl von Spreti ... died in the arachnoid region of K   Karl von Spreti was West Germany's ambassador to Guatemala during the turbulent times of the Guatemalan civil war. On March 31, 1970, he was kidnapped in Guatemala City by Fuerzas Armadas Rebeldes (FAR) guerillas. He was murdered the following week, soon after the Guatemalan government refused to negotiate his release.

211/216   *la Lisboa de los cuatro Pessoa /* for the four Pessoas, Lisbon   Montejo refers to Fernando Pessoa's four central "heteronyms": Alberto Caeiro, Ricardo Reis, Álvaro de Campos, and Bernardo Soares. Translator Richard Zenith has demonstrated that Pessoa availed himself of at least seventy-two heteronyms in his various works. See Richard Zenith, "Introduction," in *The Book of Disquietude,* by Fernando Pessoa (London: Carcanet, 1991).

222/227   *los icónicos rostros que van y vienen por la cuadra /* iconic faces come and go in the heat   I translate "*cuadra*" (which can variously mean stable, filthy space, spacious room, dormitory, and more) as "heat" here because in old-style Latin American bakeries the "*cuadra*" was the room in which the oven was located.

Bibliography

BOOKS BY EUGENIO MONTEJO

Humano paraíso. Valencia, Venezuela: Impresiones Clima, 1959.
Élegos. Caracas: Editorial Arte, 1967.
Muerte y memoria. Valencia, Venezuela: Dirección de Cultura de la Universidad de Carabobo, 1972.
La ventana oblicua. Valencia, Venezuela: Dirección de Cultura de la Universidad de Carabobo, 1974.
Algunas palabras. Caracas: Monte Ávila Editores, 1976. 2nd ed. Maracay, Venezuela: La Liebre Libre, 1995.
Terredad. Caracas: Monte Ávila Editores, 1978.
El cuaderno de Blas Coll. Caracas: Fundarte, 1981. Exp. and rev. ed. Caracas: Alfadil Ediciones, 1983.
Trópico absoluto. Caracas: Fundarte, 1982.
El taller blanco. Caracas: Fundarte, 1983. Reprinted Mexico City: Universidad Autónoma Metropolitana, Unidad Azcapotzalco, 1996.
El alfabeto del mundo. Barcelona: Editorial Laia, 1986.
Guitarra del horizonte, por Sergio Sandoval. Caracas: Alfadil Ediciones, 1991.
Adiós al siglo XX. Caracas: Ediciones Aymaria, 1992. 2nd ed. Seville: Editorial Renacimiento, 1997.
El hacha de seda. Caracas: Editorial Goliardos, 1995.
Partitura de la cigarra. Madrid: Pre-Textos, 1999.
Papiros amorosos. Madrid: Pre-Textos, 2002. 2nd ed. Caracas: Fundación Bigott, 2003.
Chamario. Caracas: Ediciones Ekaré, 2005.

La caza del relampago. In *El cuaderno de Blas Coll seguido de La caza del relampago por Lino Cervantes*. Caracas: Bid & Co. Editor, 2006.
Fábula del escriba. Madrid: Pre-Textos, 2006.

SELECTED ANTHOLOGIES

Antología. Caracas: Monte Ávila Editores, 1996.
El azul de la tierra: Antología poética. Bogotá: Norma, 1997.
Tiempo transfigurado: Antología poética. Valencia, Venezuela: Universidad de Carabobo, 2001.
Poemas selectos. Colección Poesis. Caracas: Librería Lectura, 2004.
Geometría de las horas: Una lección antológica. Edited by Adolfo Castañón. Veracruz: Universidad Veracruzana, 2006.

SELECTED CRITICISM

Cruz Pérez, Francisco José. "Eugenio Montejo: El viaje total." In *Antología*, by Eugenio Montejo. Caracas: Monte Ávila Editores, 1996.
Eyzaguirre, Luis. "Eugenio Montejo: Poesía de fin de siglo." In *Venezuela: Fin de siglo*, edited by Julio Ortega, 213–22. Caracas: Casa de Bello, 1993.
Ferrari, Américo. "Eugenio Montejo y el alfabeto del mundo." In *Alfabeto del mundo*, by Eugenio Montejo. Barcelona: Editorial Laia, 1986.
Figueredo, Juan Medina. *La terredad de Orfeo: Tensión constructiva del habla en la poesía de Eugenio Montejo*. Valencia, Venezuela: Gobierno de Carabobo, 1997.
Gomes, Miguel. "Poesía de la estación perdida: Tres aproximaciones a la lírica de Eugenio Montejo." In *El pozo de las palabras*, 99–123. Caracas: Fundarte, 1990.
———. *Poéticas del ensayo venezolano del siglo XX*, 205–10. Cranston, R.I.: Ediciones Inti, 1996.
———. "Postvanguardia y heteronimia en la poesía de Eugenio Montejo." *Hispanic Journal* 19, no. 1 (1998): 9–22.
———. "Naturaleza e historia en la poesía de Eugenio Montejo." *Revista Iberoamericana* 201 (2002): 1005–24.
———. "Eugenio Montejo's Earthdom." In *The Trees: Selected Poems 1967–2004*, by Eugenio Montejo. Translated by Peter Boyle. Cambridge, U.K.: Salt Publishing, 2004.
Guerrero, Gustavo. "La música necesaria de Eugenio Montejo." In *Geometría de las horas*, by Eugenio Montejo, 381–84. Veracruz: Universidad Veracruzana, 2006.
Gutiérrez Plaza, Arturo. "El alfabeto de la terredad: Estudio de la poética en la obra de Eugenio Montejo." *Revista Iberoamericana* 60, no. 166–67 (1994).
Hernández, Consuelo. "La arquitectura poética de Eugenio Montejo." In *Vene-*

zuela: *Fin de siglo*, edited by Julio Ortega, 223–33. Caracas: Casa de Bello, 1993.

Lasarte Valcárcel, Javier. *Sobre literatura venezolana*. Caracas: Casa de Bello, 1992.

Lastra, Pedro. "El pan y las palabras: Poesía de Eugenio Montejo." In *Catorce poetas hispanoamericanos de hoy*, edited by Pedro Lastra and Luis Eyzaguirre. Special issue, *Inti: Revista de Literatura Hispánica* 18–19 (1983–84): 211–15.

Sucre, Guillermo. *La máscara, la transparencia*. Mexico City: Fondo de Cultura Económica, 1985.

SELECTED INTERVIEWS

Bracho, Edmundo. "Respuestas para Edmundo Bracho." In *Geometría de las horas*, by Eugenio Montejo. Veracruz: Universidad Veracruzana, 2006.

Cruz Pérez, Francisco José. "Entrevista a Eugenio Montejo." In *Geometría de las horas*, by Eugenio Montejo. Veracruz: Universidad Veracruzana, 2006.

Gutiérrez, María Alejandra. "El diálogo con el enigma de Eugenio Montejo." *Literaturas: Revista Literaria Independiente de los Nuevos Tiempos* [Spain, 2002]. www.literaturas.com/EMontejoLC.htm.

López Ortega, Antonio. "Entrevista a Eugenio Montejo." In *Recital*, by Eugenio Montejo. Cuadernillo no. 8. Caracas: Espacios Unión, 1999.

López Parada, Esperanza. "La palabra en su sentido primero." *ABC Cultural* (Madrid), January 22, 2000.

Rivera, Francisco. "El cuaderno de Blas Coll." In *Ulises y el laberinto*, 71–87. Caracas: Fundarte, 1983.

———. "La poesía de Eugenio Montejo." *Inscripciones*, 87–110. Caracas: Fundarte, 1982. Reprinted in *Entre el silencio y la palabra*, by Francisco Rivera, 39–58. Caracas: Monte Ávila Editores, 1986.

TRANSLATIONS

Montejo, Eugenio. "Dos cuerpos," "Algunas palabras," "La vida," "Al fin de todo," "El Orinoco," and "Esta ciudad." Translated by Alastair Reid. In *Translation: The Journal of Literary Translation* (New York: Columbia University) 29 (Spring 1994). Special Venezuelan issue edited by Lyda Zacklin.

———. *The Trees: Selected Poems, 1967–2004*. Translated by Peter Boyle. Cambridge, U.K.: Salt Publishing, 2004.

LaVergne, TN USA
07 November 2010
203883LV00002B/2/P